# 52 RED PILLS

# 52 RED PILLS

## A NEW-AGE PLAYBOOK TO BECOME HEALTHY, WEALTHY AND WISE

Eika Chaturvedi Banerjee

&

Siddharth Banerjee

PAN

First published 2020 by Pan
an imprint of Pan Macmillan Publishing India Private Limited
707, Kailash Building,
26, K. G. Marg, New Delhi – 110 001
www.panmacmillan.co.in

Pan Macmillan, 6 Briset St, Farringdon, London EC1M 5NR
Associated companies throughout the world
www.panmacmillan.com

ISBN 978-93-89109-27-6



1 3 5 7 9 8 6 4 2



Typeset in Sabon LT Std by R. Ajith Kumar, New Delhi
Printed and bound in India by Thomson Press India Ltd.

*To the two Shaktis,*
*Oishee and Tavishee*
*As they continue to learn.*

# CONTENTS

# PREFACE

## WHAT INSPIRED US?

We have both been *passionate hyper-learners* our entire lives – through school, college, our MBA days together, our corporate careers over the past twenty years and overall in life. When faced with a situation, both of us would always seek to enquire, learn, distil and then act (wisely or unwisely so), rather than wait to get answers from somewhere or to follow an existing paradigm.

One of the principles that has helped us gain success in our fields is the *discipline of self-learning*, which is said to be the highest level of activity from a return on investment (ROI) perspective. This continuous journey of self-learning has helped us evolve as people and as leaders. It has not only enhanced our self-awareness and our ability to connect with others, but also expanded our perspectives on life and success.

And while we have imbibed knowledge and experience along our four decades on Earth, we have also come to realize how little we still know. Hence, on the New Year's Eve of 2018, sitting amidst the lush green environs of a tiger reserve, we decided to take our journey of self-learning into the next orbit!

We chose to embark on a unique *52 Weeks Learning Challenge*. For this, we ambitiously penned down a long list of 63 actions or subjects we would cover across the 52 weeks of 2018. The fundamental idea behind this endeavour was simple: we would completely immerse ourselves into ONE TOPIC EVERY WEEK.

The topics we listed were the ones that deeply interested us. Diverse and fascinating, they covered a vast gamut of ideas and themes: from the art of making fine coffee to mind maps, from how billionaires think to how pro-marathoners train, from mindfulness to muay-thai, and from ancient medicine practices to cutting-edge haematology.

This accelerated self-learning was a three-step process.

a) We would speak to experts and hack into their life-journeys and learnings.
b) We would scan and absorb existing literature on the subjects (both ancient knowledge and latest research papers), thus building up an information database.
c) We would debate and discuss these concepts in great detail between ourselves to understand them. The idea being to find interconnections in the knowledge we had accumulated in order to uncover new insights and appreciate fresh perspectives.

To make all this possible in a disciplined manner, we had to prioritize our time ruthlessly, given that we both work in demanding corporate roles, and spend our leisure time with our two daughters, as well as our family and friends. Hence, we drew up a 'Sacrifice List' that basically axed certain activities to make time for this weekly discipline of self-learning. Binge-watching shows and movies on Netflix was now a thing of the past. We even cut down on attending corporate parties to once a week. And so on.

Lastly, to create a memorable hook for our #52WeeksLearningChallenge, we drew inspiration from Morpheus in the movie *Matrix*, who offers Neo the choice of taking the blue or the red pill. The latter denotes an adventure across uncharted paths, and so, we have named our hyper-learning journey across 52 weeks of 2018 as '52RedPills'.

While this book is about our journey, we invite you to embark on your very own 'RedPills' journey. You're certain to be surprised and fascinated by what you find along the way!

# CREATING YOUR OWN 52REDPILLS JOURNEY

Everyone's journey is unique. Ours certainly was. And we hope as you read this book, you will get some nuggets of learnings, tips and hacks from our experiences that are relevant to you.

As you consider taking that first exciting step towards your own adventure, and before you begin hyper-learning, here's a brief process note with five questions for you to define your learning journey:

1. What do you love most about yourself as an individual/couple/team/family?

    ________________________________________

    ________________________________________

    ________________________________________

2. What did you enjoy doing (alone/together) the most?

    ________________________________________

    ________________________________________

    ________________________________________

3. What are the themes (cuisines, travel, dancing, wines, movies, literature and sports are a few examples) you want to explore (alone/together)?

________________________________________

________________________________________

________________________________________

5. How do you want to explore yourself/your togetherness/ your themes? For instance, would you like to cook experimental meals, learn new dances, play sports, watch and analyze movies, explore newer workouts, and so on?

________________________________________

________________________________________

________________________________________

5. What is your long list of seventy things you want to do, learn about, practice, and/or create?

________________________________________

________________________________________

________________________________________

Draw up a simple table, as shown below, to map out your resources and assign responsibilities.

| S. No. | Topic | Category | Expert | Resources | Responsibility |
|---|---|---|---|---|---|
| 1 | Sleep | Health | Arianna H | Ancient texts + research | Sid |
| 2 | Meditation | Wisdom | Art of Living | Ancient texts + research | Eika |
| 3 | Decoding the Bhagwad Gita | Wisdom | Sadhu/Guru | Classes + expert recordings + videos | Eika |
| 4 | Gratitude | Wisdom | People who have beaten the odds | Ancient texts + research | Eika |
| 5 | Creativity | Wisdom | Agency CEO | Research papers + books | Sid |
| 6 | Martial Arts | Inter-related | Sensei/ Experts | Classes + expert recordings + videos | Sid & Eika |
| 7 | Beat a Heart Attack | Health | Doctors' Panel | Medical whitepapers + latest research | Sid |

Choose a day that suits you (every Saturday, Sunday, Monday, or whichever day works for you), and then, at the end of every week of the coming year, do the following exercise on that day.

## EXERCISE

- Tick off the item/topic you covered from your list.
- Create your own log and record of what you did, how you did, what you learnt, and what you would like to do again.
- Maintain it also in the form of photographs, written experiences in your journal or diary, videos, on your social media feeds, and/or at the end of every RedPill in this book.

And towards the end of the year, you will have your own 52RedPills journey compilation, filled with shared experiences and wonderful memories to keep you company as you evolve yourself.

Through the year, you will have learned, laughed, fallen, recovered, shared, created, danced, evolved and oh so much more.

You will have explored.

You will have lived.

# SUMMARY OF OUR 52REDPILLS JOURNEY OVER 52 WEEKS

Week 1 – Good **Sleep**
Week 2 – The **Art of Thinking**
Week 3 – The Science of **Food**
Week 4 – The Spice of Life: **Cinnamon**
Week 5 – Decoding **Culture**
Week 6 – On **Mindfulness**
Week 7 – The Science of **Symbols and Rituals**
Week 8 – Rock **Under Pressure**
Week 9 – The Next Orbit of **Leadership**
Week 10 – **Power Mornings**
Week 11 – **Spirituality** as a Superpower
Week 12 – Going **Organic**
Week 13 – Hacking **Martial Arts**
Week 14 – Turning Curiosity into **Creativity**
Week 15 – From Where on Earth Do You **Draw Your Energy?**
Week 16 – Boost Your **Memory Power**
Week 17 – The Magical World of **Whiskey**
Week 18 – On **Life Hacks**
Week 19 – Be a **Super Woman**
Week 20 – Start a **Movement**

# AUTHORS' NOTE

Our 52 weeks' journey across 2018 was intense and hectic, covering a host of topics that would (hopefully) help us become 'healthy, wealthy, and wise', as we integrated learnings from ancient wisdom along with modern-day expertise.

To give us a breather from some of the more intense themes, we incorporated some lighter weeks in between, where we delved into experiential topics such as whiskey, coffee, etc. These experiences can never be evocatively captured in a book chapter; hence, we have kept these specific RedPills crisp and with names edited or changed on request.

---

WEEK 1

# GOOD SLEEP

*'Sleep that knits up the raveled sleave of care,*
*The death of each day's life, sore labor's bath,*
*Balm of hurt minds, great nature's second course,*
*Chief nourisher in life's feast.'*

*MACBETH*, WILLIAM SHAKESPEARE

## THE CONTEXT

Our research area in our first week of 52RedPills was GOOD SLEEP as a key factor for our well being and happiness.

Why good sleep, you might ask?

The backstory is as follows. Eika and I (Siddharth) completed our MBA as the Class of 2000 at FMS-Delhi and joined the corporate sector. One of our first memories about the vicissitudes of the rat race was the news of a super-achieving corporate star, then president of a large IT company, who died at the age of 40 from a massive heart attack. Media reports said that lack of sleep led to body under stress which was the reason for the sudden, unfortunate demise of an individual, who otherwise followed a sensible diet and regular exercise schedule. Over the years, we heard the same story, with some variations, numerous times, as people we knew suffered similar outcomes.

And since we both turned 40 this year, issues related to health and well being are pretty much top-of-mind for us.

## THE PROCESS

We began by reading deeply on this subject, with texts ranging from our ancient Vedas to the latest articles, including the immensely interesting 2017 *New York Times* article, 'Sleep as the Status Symbol'. Through all of these, good sleep emerged as a critical part of the well-being regimen to help avoid sudden stress to the human body. And we realized that while awareness regarding the importance of good sleep was increasing, a disciplined way of approaching this was required. Our online browsing also revealed that new industries were being built around the concept of providing a good sleep experience – from sleep pods and aromatherapy to technology products for aiding sleep. One of the global voices shaping this conversation is Arianna Huffington, who has established a new company called Thrive Global, with India as the second launch market after the US.

And here is where we got lucky. It turned out that Arianna was visiting Mumbai. Introduced via a friend of a friend, we were fortunate to spend some quality time with her over a dinner and take in her thoughts on good sleep.

In the same week, Eika met up with her Rishi-*ji* and gleaned some nuggets of timeless wisdom by a deep discussion of this topic. Overall, thus, we were able to get some deep insights into the nature of our minds and our sleep states.

In summary, the body–mind conflict between alertness and rest has the following four manifestations:

- **Jagrut Awastha or Awake State:** This is how we lead our daily lives, hyper and frenetic in body and sharply alert in the mind. There is no rest, and so the body fatigues and the mind tires.
- **Supt Awastha or Sleep State:** This is the tired state of deep sleep. When the body is at rest, and there's no awareness or alertness of the mind.
- **Swapna Awastha or Dream State:** This is the fevered mind-and-body state of the restless, dreamful sleep. The body awakens exhausted and unrested, and the mind is in a foggy haze of uncertainty. There is neither physical rest, nor any alertness or awareness of the mind.
- **Turiya Awastha or Alpha State:** This is the state of conscious clarity of meditation. The body is in effortless, calm rest, and the mind has absolute clarity, alertness and awareness, and is in the present.

It is a fact that given the hectic lives we all lead, which involve erratic sleeping patterns, late nights and red-eye flights, we would all benefit immensely from learning to deep-rest. And do consider how infinitely productive, efficient, brilliant and resonant we all would be if we could exist forever in the Turiya State.

And it is possible to do so. As Eika realized, you need to **Meditate, Breathe, and Be.**

## THE LEARNINGS

1) Eight hours of sleep every night is a must. It enhances productivity and creativity. It is important to get the right quantity of deep or REM sleep within these hours in order to wake up fresh.

2) You can increase your focus and powers of concentration dramatically in the Alpha State.
3) Sleeping between 10:30 p.m. and 1:30 a.m. is critical. Your liver needs this time to replenish itself. It is also beneficial to have regular, fixed times to go to sleep and to wake up. Sleep likes habit.

Eika and I experimented with some of these learnings during the week. Eika discovered that meditating just before going to bed allowed her to enjoy a deep, peaceful sleep. I nursed my liver by trying to go to bed earlier. It wasn't as easy as I expected it to be. Detoxing from devices was probably the toughest part. Nevertheless, what certainly needs a mention is that on days that we tucked ourselves in early, we woke up refreshed, recharged and completely energized.

## RESOURCES

- *The Sleep Revolution: Transforming Your Life, One Night at a Time* by Arianna Huffington
- Check out: www.thriveglobal.com for more on Arianna Huffington and her work.

An interesting video to watch by *The Economist*, 'What Happens When We Sleep?'

## TO THINK AND DO THIS WEEK

### THINK

What has been that one healthy, good sleep habit you have been trying to cultivate?

___

___

___

### DO

Try to disconnect from all online or communication devices at night, an hour before you sleep, for at least one week. In other words, keep your devices outside the bedroom and stay away from your phone/s at least an hour BEFORE your sleep time.

Experience:

___

___

___

Learnings:

___

___

___

Challenges:

___

___

___

WEEK 2

# THE ART OF THINKING

*'Thinking: the talking of the soul with itself.'*

PLATO

## THE CONTEXT

Our research area for this week was on THE ART OF THINKING. This is a hot topic for us, especially because the world around us is changing so fast. As they say, we are living in a VUCA world – one that is Volatile, Unpredictable, Chaotic and Ambiguous. Such conditions naturally force us to reassess our assumptions and adapt to new operating conditions. We, thus, researched the fluency of developing mental models, understanding patterns, connecting dots, figuring out the value of being interdisciplinary. In essence, we attempted the art of honing our ability to fully open our minds.

## THE PROCESS

This week's quest took us on an interesting journey as we meandered across wisdom from ancient literature and a lunch meeting with one of India's prominent tech-entrepreneurs, to some insights from an online course on cutting-edge design thinking.

I spent time with Kunal Shah, one of India's foremost internet entrepreneurs, philosopher, fabulously provocative thinker, and the founder of Freecharge and CRED. Our one-hour coffee meeting turned into a three-hour-long, intellectually stimulating lunch discussion. Two of the most fascinating things Kunal did post his Freecharge venture was to extensively travel the world and read exhaustively. This exploration allowed him to look at the world from first principles and inspired him to see interconnections across diverse subjects. For instance, the principles of similarities between Hinduism and Blockchain were a fascinating provocation that he shared with us.

We also signed up for and blitz-completed a Design Thinking e-course from IDEO, one of the world's foremost global design companies, at the forefront of creating change through design. It is also one of the leading organizations for online resources with tests and courses to stimulate your creative juices.

In the meantime, Eika dove into texts ranging from *Mandukya Upanishada* to some translated age-old texts by recent philosophers for an ancient wisdom perspective. And through her study of Hindu philosophy, she came across the concept of *antah-karna* (the inner cause).

Her understanding of this ancient concept is as follows: the mind collects raw data through our senses that engage and transact with our environment. This raw data is collected through sight, touch, taste, hearing, smell, our behaviour, our conscious mind, and our persona – this level of the mind is known as the *manas*. Think of it as the RAM of computing.

Through the layers of the subconscious, these raw strands

of data get processed into information. This is done through the processors of the *chitta* (memory), *vivek* and *buddhi* (analysis and judgement), and *aham* (ego). These strands of information then become available to us and are accessed as and when required. Think of this as your computer's hard disk or CPU.

To express this as an example, imagine the five-year-old you got burnt by hot tea. This experience was 'collected' by your *manas* through the transaction of sight and touch. It was then processed through your five-year-old *buddhi* into information organized as 'dangerous'. The 25-year-old you now recalls this information through your *chitta* every time you are tempted to consume hot tea, thereby alerting you to exercise caution.

So, indulge your senses as you experience the world and the *manas*, and allow your *chitta*, *vivek*, *buddhi* and *aham* to soak in, massage and organize the data you collect.

## THE LEARNINGS

1) Our minds have four functionalities – *manas, chitta, buddhi and aham*. The full potential engagement of the mind is achieved only when all four are activated. The superficial mind operates only from one or two of this consciousness.
2) Meta themes are a passion for Kunal. These emerge once you increase your understanding of the world – join the dots (everything is connected, especially in today's digital world) – and probe the *why*. Hence, our learning was about the fascinating interrelationships that get revealed once you join the dots in seemingly disparate subjects.

3) A recurring theme for promoting creative thinking is the process of Rapid Prototyping. This process involves creating a simple visualization, such as a sketch, to describe an infant idea. Early feedback then helps to shape the idea more articulately. This is followed by getting a base concept out to the audience.

### RESOURCES

- Check out online courses at www.Ideo.com
- Learn more about Design Thinking from online courses at Stanford and MIT.
- *Frugal Innovation: How to do More with Less* by Navi Radjou and Jaideep Prabhu
- *Breakout Nations: In Pursuit of the Next Economic Miracles* by Ruchir Sharma

## TO THINK AND DO THIS WEEK

### THINK

What subjects have always fascinated you? What have you always been curious about?

### DO

Use the fabulous tool of Mind Maps to see interconnections between different knowledge sets.

Experience:

Learnings:

Challenges:

# WEEK 3

# THE SCIENCE OF FOOD

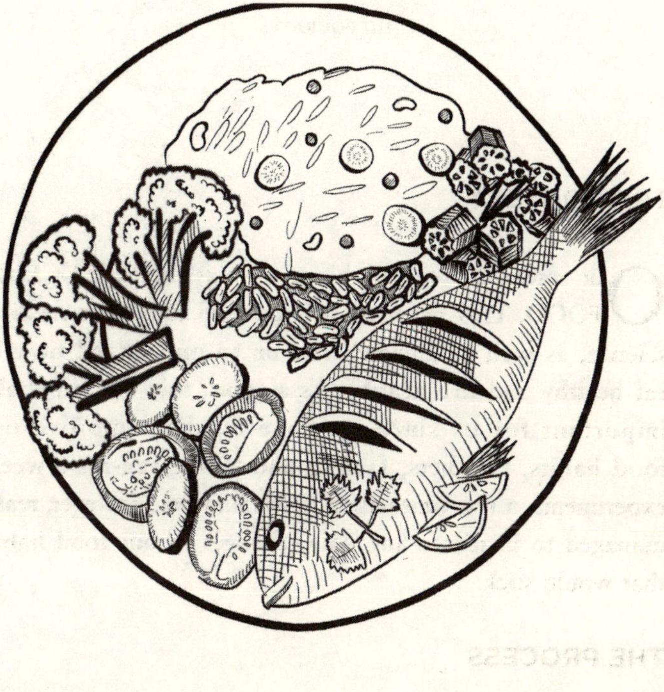

*'Let food be thy medicine,*
*Thy medicine shall be thy food.'*

HIPPOCRATES

## THE CONTEXT

Our research area for this week was the SCIENCE OF FOOD. This required delving into the latest medical science, as well as ancient wisdom to understand how to eat healthy and live healthy. As a topic, this was especially important for us since we have tried to improve our food habits, via diets, fasting and 'going-veg-for-a-week' experiments, a few times already. We had not, however, really managed to inculcate any daily changes in our food habits that would stick.

## THE PROCESS

Eika and I decided to explore the translated writings on various foods and their impact as described under the yogic and Ayurvedic systems, and seeing what we could put into use. In addition to our studies, I spent some productive hours in discussion with Anuj Rakyan, a former athlete and the founder and managing director of Raw Pressery, to learn from his expert insights on food.

Finally, as a quasi-test of our recently acquired knowledge, Eika and I hosted a live Twitter chat session (courtesy our friends at @LnM) on 'Good Food & Good Living', and put our learnings to use while getting real time feedback and more know-how from our listeners.

## THE LEARNINGS

1) Over the ages, food cultures across the world have figured out that all diet needs to be balanced. This means that all food groups need to feature in your meals. Rajma-chawal, daal-roti, and fish-n-chips are just a few simple examples of protein and carb combinations. Do consider this premise before starting Atkins, Keto or any other fad diet of modern times. Also, always consume locally grown and eaten foods. So, aloo-paranthas loaded with butter is ideal in Punjab, whereas idli and coconut chutney are best suited to coastal Kerala.
2) We have all heard of 'an apple a day keeps the doctor away' and 'a banana in the morning takes care of acidity and controls blood sugar all day' advice. There are similar health benefits in nuts too, so make sure to keep a jar of healthy nuts at home, office, and even in your car.
3) It is fascinating how the respiratory system (the *naadis*) operates and offers signals regarding our food and drink intake. How? Well, check your breathing. If your left nostril is more active, it is time to consume fluids; and if your right nostril is more active, that is the body's signal to eat solid food.

**Fun Fact:** *Ayurveda = the Knowledge of Life*

Based on our learnings during this week, we made three small yet critical changes to our lifestyle. First, Eika and I ensured that we inculcate the habit of an early dinner, preferably by 7 p.m., along with our kids, at a device-free dinner table. Second, we have drastically reduced our intake of processed sugar in tea or coffee and food. And lastly, we ensure portion control, hence, smaller servings of food on the table with a balanced diet of all the things we love eating, from carbs to proteins.

## RESOURCES

- *Climbing the Mango Trees: A Memoir of a Childhood in India* by Madhur Jaffrey
- *A Cook's Tour: Global Adventures in Extreme Cuisines* and *No Reservations: Around the World on an Empty Stomach* by Antony Bourdain
- *Rude Food: The Collected Food Writings of Vir Sanghvi* by Vir Sanghvi

## TO THINK AND DO THIS WEEK

### THINK

What are your 'mood' foods? These include comfort, childhood, stress, party, snack, sad, and happy foods, among others.

### DO

Try eliminating white foods from your consumption this week. This means no white flour (maida and bread included), white rice or white sugar.

Experience:

Learnings:

Challenges:

WEEK 4

# THE SPICE OF LIFE: CINNAMON

*'And still she slept an azure-lidded sleep,*
*In blanched linen, smooth, and lavender'd,*
*While he from forth the closet brought a heap*
*Of candied apple, quince, and plum, and gourd;*
*With jellies soother than the creamy curd,*
*And lucent syrops, tinct with cinnamon;*
*Manna and dates, in argosy transferr'd*
*From Fez; and spiced dainties, every one,*
*From silken Samarcand to cedar'd Lebanon.'*

'THE EVE OF ST AGNES' BY JOHN KEATS

## THE CONTEXT

Our research area this week arose from the enquiry into Ayurveda and well being last week. It enticed us to delve deeper into the SPICE OF LIFE, namely CINNAMON.

## THE PROCESS

This week's journey involved exploring both ancient medical texts and having conversations with doctors and experts regarding this special spice. While Eika looked into our traditional food systems and the role of spices within that, I undertook a trip to Sri Lanka, the 'Cinnamon Isle', to speak to various entrepreneurs and Ayurvedic practitioners about this wonder spice. Fortunately, this fell perfectly in line with a personal trip to meet my friends in Colombo and Galle.

## THE LEARNINGS

Although we just managed to scratch the surface of this vast topic, here are the three key takeaways from our experience:

1) There is a marked difference between Western and Indian classifications of food. The former operates on the basis of the chemical compounds in the food: protein (amino acids and building blocks), carbohydrates (sugars and energy providers), vitamins and minerals (enzymes and facilitators), fats and oils (lubricators), fibre (roughage) and water.

   In ancient Indian science, however, food is classified more holistically to include its integration with the specific human body that consumes it. This takes the form of *rasa panchaka*, which comprises the five factors of a *dravya* (substance). These are: *rasa* or taste, *guna* or qualities, *vipaka* or taste conversion after digestion, *veerya* or potency, and *prabhava* or the special effect of the food. This allows for herbs and spices to be included and studied among the foods, unlike the western compound classification.
2) Cinnamon has significant medical properties. For instance, half a teaspoon of cinnamon per day is said to lower cholesterol. It has an anti-clotting effect, as well. In a study conducted at Copenhagen University, patients who were given half a teaspoon of this powder, combined with

a tablespoon of honey, every morning before breakfast experienced a marked relief in arthritis pain after one week.* Smelling cinnamon also boosts cognitive function and memory. And it is a great source of manganese, fibre, iron and calcium, too.

3) The almost magical medicinal properties of cinnamon have ensured it an enduring appeal through the ages. In Roman times, cinnamon was considered more valuable than gold! For centuries, the source of cinnamon was a mystery to the Western world. Today, there are four main cinnamon producers in the world: China, Vietnam, Indonesia and Sri Lanka. The cinnamon (species *cinnamomum verum*) found in Sri Lanka is considered the best since it has the lowest levels of coumarin (which is said to cause liver and kidney damage in high concentration).

What makes cinnamon even more versatile is that it can be consumed in a variety of ways. Sprinkle powdered cinnamon over your steaming cup of cappuccino or latte. Or add a stick to your broth, soup or curry. Cinnamon boiled water can be used as syrup to soften and sweeten your cakes. Boil it with nutmeg, clove and pepper, and add a generous dose of it to your brandy for the perfect winter evening Toddy. Or simply add a stick for the most flavourful biryani ever.

**Overall summary**: Add some spice to your life!

*NOTE: These are our personal interpretations and should not be construed as medical advice. These serve as thought starters*

* Team, News. 'Researchers Pursuing Arthritis Protein.' Københavns Universitet. Accessed November 16, 2019. https://news.ku.dk/all_news/2014/01/researchers-pursuing-arthritis-protein/.

*for anyone who is interested in this area. We encourage you to do your own research and come to conclusions and actions independently.*

**Fun Fact:** *During our research, we came across a new term – cinnamon words. As we all know, many authors, and indeed some public speakers, have a tendency to use certain words statistically more often than others. These are known as cinnamon words, as the data journalist Ben Blatt memorably dubbed them in his 2017 book,* Nabokov's Favorite Word is Mauve: What the Numbers Reveal About the Classics, Bestsellers, and Our Own Writing. *In Hindi, these are colloquially known as* takeeya kalaams*!*

## RESOURCES

- Some interesting cinnamon-based recipes can be found at www.Curejoy.com
  A host of online resources exist for more informed discussions on cinnamon.

## TO THINK AND DO THIS WEEK

### THINK

What food journeys have you undertaken to discover exotic or exceptionally good food?

### DO

Experiment with your favourite ingredients and spices to create some interesting food this week.

Experience:

Learnings:

Challenges:

WEEK 5

# DECODING CULTURE

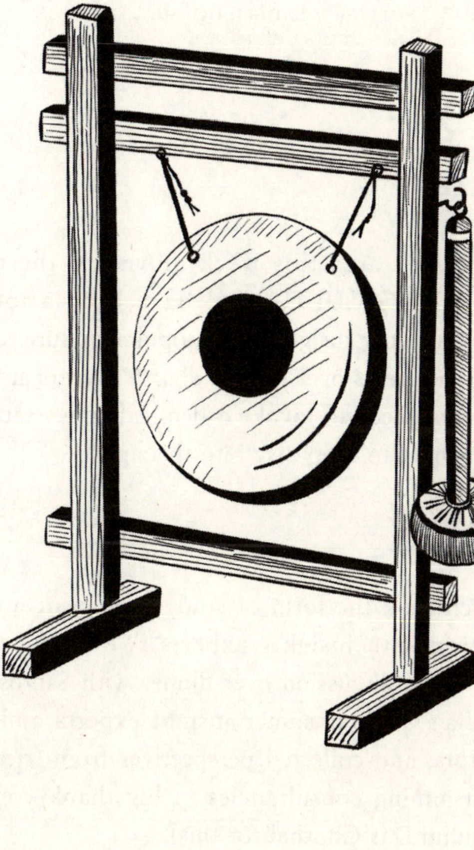

*'A moment's insight is sometimes worth a life's experience.'*

OLIVER WENDELL HOLMES, SR

## THE CONTEXT

Our research area this week moved to the topic of DECODING CULTURE. I have been a long-term student of consumer insights and popular culture and have learnt from the greats over my (Siddharth's) years at Unilever and, hence, was keen to invoke a detailed conversation with Eika who wanted to deep dive into this area.

## THE PROCESS

Our research took the form of studying ancient mythology and speaking with insights experts. We jammed over a fabulous evening discussion over dinner with Santosh Desai, one of India's best consumer insight experts and culture commentators, and collected perspectives from friends who run insight-mining consultancies (a big thank you to our friend, Nandini Das Ghoshal for this).

## THE LEARNINGS

1) Every myth, value and belief is represented through a symbol, story, or ritual. In order to understand people or glean insights into their behaviours and attitudes, one needs to hear their stories, celebrate their festivals, participate in their rituals and study their symbols. Ask and observe till you've figured out their belief systems, to the point of predictability.

   *Note: We will delve more into the concept of Blood DNA in subsequent RedPills.*

2) According to one of our experts, insights are about making the familiar a little unfamiliar! Hence, a good insight should blow your mind and ideally cause a change in perspective or a shift in meaning. We debated using a powerful insight about the smoking epidemic – one that does not start from the problem, but from the solution.

   *Note: One of the best anti-smoking strategies has been highlighting the concept of passive smoking. This converts a private matter into an interpersonal or societal issue.*

3) We also discussed interesting questions from an insight lens. Why is a courtroom built like a play-acting stage? How did the polio immunization program succeed in India? Why is it okay to wear a bikini on a hotel beach and not to the same property's reception, a few metres away? What does a 'Fall Collection' even mean in India? How can companies tap into 'desi' and build fabulous brands?

The key learning was how brands (and celebrities) can use symbols and gestures to increase impact?

We discussed these and more questions around 'How Meaning Gets Created' via semiotics and popular culture.

**RESOURCES**

- *Mother Pious Lady: Making Sense of Everyday India* by Santosh Desai
- *We Are Like That Only: Understanding the Logic of Consumer India* by Rama Bijapurkar
- Writings of Mary Douglas and Roland Barthes

## TO THINK AND DO THIS WEEK

### THINK

What attracts you about the ones you love and like?

### DO

Revisit your favourite childhood books and comics, and read them with your now adult perspective.

Experience:

Learnings:

Challenges:

WEEK 6

# ON MINDFULNESS

*'There are only two ways to live your life.*
*One is as though nothing is a miracle.*
*The other is as though everything is a miracle.'*

ALBERT EINSTEIN

## THE CONTEXT

Our research area this week was devoted to MINDFULNESS. We would qualify this effort as being at the beginner's level, especially given the scope and complexity of this subject. The provocation for us to learn about it came from the hectic, mad lives that we have led in the corporate world, and our search for balance and equanimity in our lives.

## THE PROCESS

We spent a couple of evenings attempting to interpret the knowledge provided in the Vedas on this topic. We also spoke with a modern-day monk, and fast-read literature ranging from that written by famed international psychologist Daniel Goleman to the posts by super-blogger Mark Manson for a diverse array of perspectives.

The benefits from the practice of mindfulness also came alive from the personal experiences of Eishita Chaturvedi, who also is Eika's sister. A practitioner of Nichiren Buddhism, Eishita is a trained singer, ex-NDTV journalist, gifted storyteller and the founder of a mom's talent marketplace, MomsCanDo. You can find her on the MomsCanDo Facebook page, MomsCanDo vlogs on Instagram, and as Eishita Chaturvedi on YouTube for her lovely music renditions.

'Ten years ago,' says Eishita, 'when I went for my first Soka Gakkai meeting, where everyone practised Nichiren Buddhism, the one aspect that truly stuck with me, was the simultaneity of the cause-and-effect law. Essentially, when I wake up, when I sleep, when I emote, when I speak, every action is manifesting an effect. Not somewhere distant, but right there, that very moment.

Now imagine living with that kind of mindfulness at all times. Frankly, it's not just difficult. It's not humanly possible. And that is where the daily practise of chanting *Nam Myoho Renge Kyo* comes in. It is the faith that works, when you take action, when you take responsibility, when every time, it guides you from within, about all that you do, at the start and end of the day.

This practise is often confused with meditation. However, Nichiren Buddhism and the process of chanting is actually a conversation with your highest life state – that of Buddhahood. Each time, involving all our senses, the mind, to paint and imagine the best picture of what your existence can be, constantly putting in the finest details: the mouth, which says the chant loud enough for you to hear it and goes back through your ears; the eyes, which are open in conversation with your Buddha potential; and the sense of everything being in action at all times.

It taught me to constantly have hope. A hope that is not passive, but an all-encompassing and active one. A hope that arises from the depths of our existence, by knowing that I am in control and I will win – a constant reminder, at every moment, *no matter what*!

This practise taught me to grow every moment, amidst every trial, tribulation and victory. You start living the practise when you express gratitude for all that you have every time, coupled with the determination for all that you will achieve. Through it all, establishing the beautiful concept of "Human Revolution", which is a revolt against all things dark within me, and seeing the smallest changes everyday, with a very elevated sense of perceiving your own and another's life.'

## THE LEARNINGS

While we learnt some aspects of mindfulness, it is safe to say there is a substantial amount of experiential practise required to really understand this subject. Meanwhile, our three quick takeaways are:

1) The idea of mindfulness, in life coaching, is also known as 'processing in the present'. Being in the here and now. The human 'monkey mind' alternates between the anger or hurt of the past and the fear or anxiety of the future. During this state of being, the present moment disappears unlived, contributing to the vicious circle of more hurt, anger and stress.
2) Yoga helps you with *your* kind of mindfulness. The Yoga of Synthesis talks of four kinds of yoga to suit one's temperament: Karma Yoga (based on action), Jnana Yoga (based on will, intellect and knowledge), Bhakti Yoga (based on emotion and surrender), and Raja Yoga (based

on control over mental and physical energy). The objective here is to pick your form of yoga as per your temperament. And then immerse in every single transaction, interaction and experience through the lens of your karma, jnana, bhakti and raja, with complete and absolute awareness of every single living and waking moment.

3) Why should you consider mindfulness? Well, it's a good option if you are seeking to be effective at work and happy in life. Mindfulness has proven to not only enhance mental performance and help you make better decisions, but also help develop more fruitful relationships. So, put away your phone occasionally, take notes, ask questions to clarify and be consciously in the zone of empathy. Consider getting off what we like to call the 'Hedonic Treadmill'.

And here's a tantalizing query for you. While you may have an idea of what it takes to make you happy, do you know what trade-offs or sacrifices you are prepared to make for achieving that happiness? Give it a think.

## RESOURCES

- *The Buddha in Daily Life: An Introduction to the Buddhism of Nichiren Daishonin* by Richard Causton
- 'Why Mindfulness is a Super Power', a video on YouTube. It's a fantastic animation on mindfulness.
- The official website of Soka Gakkai, **www.sgi.org**, is quite interesting and informative. It covers the experiences of its members, and relates how they practised to improve their lives and be mindful victors everyday.
- *The Miracle of Mindfulness* by Thich Nhat Hanh

## TO THINK AND DO THIS WEEK

### THINK

What gives you happiness? What makes you happy? When are you the happiest?

### DO

Try to engage and be there in every situation. Talk to your taxi or car driver, your maid, your neighbour, or even a friendly stranger in the elevator. Listen to them actively.

Experience:

Learnings:

Challenges:

WEEK 7

# THE SCIENCE OF SYMBOLS AND RITUALS

*'A ritual is the enactment of a myth.*
*And, by participating in the ritual, you are participating in the myth.*
*And since myth is a projection of the depth wisdom of the psyche,*
*By participating in a ritual, participating in the myth,*
*You are being, as it were, put in accord with that wisdom,*
*Which is the wisdom that is inherent within you anyhow.*
*Your consciousness is being reminded of the wisdom of your own life.*
*I think ritual is terribly important.'*

JOSEPH CAMPBELL

## THE CONTEXT

Our discussion this week, partly prompted by the frequent questions by our daughters on why we follow certain traditions and rituals in India, made us delve into this area in detail. Do we follow certain rituals because they are connected to religious beliefs? Do our rituals have an underlying rationale? We set up fact-finding missions amongst us, and this week saw the Banerjee household feverishly discussing and debating on the topic of THE SCIENCE OF RITUALS AND SYMBOLS.

## THE PROCESS

Interestingly, back in 2017–18, Eika had already engaged in a substantial amount of research when she started sharing nuggets on our rituals and symbols inspired by ancient wisdom on a biweekly radio segment called 'Uncommon Sense' with RJ Siddharth. That helped to a certain degree as we now sat down and had detailed discussions on why we follow certain rituals in India. And most of the information below comes from Eika's preparation for her radio segments, which resonated strongly with her listeners and afforded her a substantial followership for six quarters as she shared perspective on the show.

Frankly, we were amazed at the underlying science behind some of our practices. And, in the process, it was truly wonderful to know deeper about our heritage. More often than not, that which has become superstition today was once actually a well thought through 'scientific' practice. All values and beliefs manifest themselves through stories, symbols and rituals. Over years and millennia of societal practice, however, contexts change, and the logic and rationale *behind* these practices are lost. And so, if we ever seek to understand people and culture, and, therefore, even ourselves, we need to peel back the layers of our stories, decode our symbols and deep dive into understanding our rituals.

## THE LEARNINGS

1) As mentioned above, our values and beliefs get manifested through our stories and rituals. Our mythology then becomes the most tangible unit of our blood memory. For instance, the famous story of the Dashavataar (the

ten primary incarnations of God Vishnu) is the manifest expression of our understanding of human evolution, as per Hindu mythology. From the first avatar, Matsya (the Piscean fish), to the second, Kurma (half-man, half-turtle), to Varaha (the boar), then Narasimha (part-lion, part-man), then Vamana (the dwarf human), to Parasurama (the saint-warrior), to Rama, then Krishna, to the Buddha, and finally to Kalki (the destroyer and recreator). Each of these represents the varying stages of the human race. Many centuries later, Charles Darwin enunciated similar principles with his natural evolution theories. Hence, it is amazing to see the interconnections between different eras and cultures.

2) We spoke about symbolism in our rituals and how we can use that to understand our actions in today's life. The symbolism behind the River Ganga was particularly interesting. In Hinduism, Ganga is revered as a goddess and the consort of Lord Vishnu, a mother, provider, nurturer, the pure, a giver of shelter, a deliverer from and destroyer of sins, and the absorber of death. This made us appreciate the reason why millions of devotees take a dip in this holy river, and also why cremations take place on its banks in Varanasi. It also shows us, potentially, how this cultural understanding could be factored into policy-making and urban planning for cities in India, the 'Safaayee Abhyaan' ('clean the river' initiatives).

3) Our meandering discussions also led us to the science behind these rituals. For instance, did you know that bending to touch someone's feet, in addition to being a gesture of respect, is rooted in medical science since it elongates one's spine and, thus, prolongs one's lifespan? Hence, there is scientific truth behind the blessings of elders

for a long life (*jug jug jiyo* and *jeete raho*) when you greet them by touching their feet.

Also, consider the ritual of applying *tilak* on someone's forehead before an important task, such as before going out to battle or starting a journey. The act of applying the *tilak* is believed to activate the pineal gland, which is the seat of human judgment, the *ajna chakra* (the third-eye *chakra*) where *buddhi* and *vivek* (judgement and analysis) sit, which brings one's mind into focus for the task ahead.

For us, the learning this week was valuable in two ways: first, it reinforced our belief in our rituals, ensuring that we follow a certain process based on a certain underlying rationale and, hence, anchored us further to our culture and way of life. Second, we were able to share these learnings with our daughters and pass on the knowledge on our rich culture and rituals.

## RESOURCES

- *Hindu Rites and Rituals: Where They Come from and What They Mean* by K. V. Singh
- *Why I Am a Hindu* by Shashi Tharoor
- Check out more references and learnings at www.vedantaworld.org if you want to learn more.

## TO THINK AND DO THIS WEEK

### THINK

What were some non-negotiable rituals as you were growing up? What importance do they have for you?

______

______

______

### DO

Create your own symbol, one that represents you, and build a little ritual around it.

______

______

______

Experience:

______

______

Learnings:

______

______

Challenges:

______

______

WEEK 8

# ROCK UNDER PRESSURE

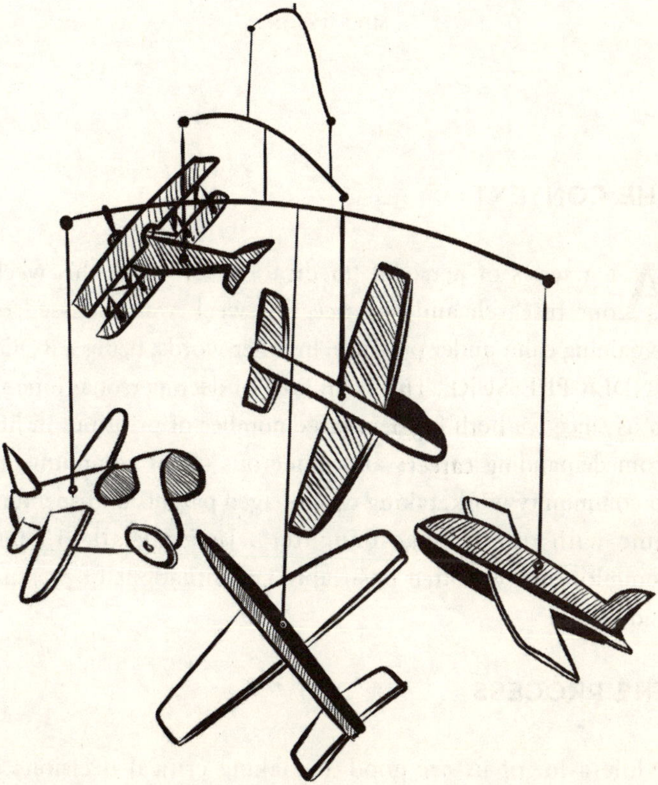

*'Everyone has a plan till they get punched in the face.'*

MIKE TYSON

## THE CONTEXT

As a series of personal (medical) crises hit us this week, our research and practice this week was focussed on remaining calm under pressure. In other words, being a ROCK UNDER PRESSURE. This is an area of deep personal interest to us since we both juggle a large number of priorities in life, from demanding careers and numerous social commitments, to community work, taking care of aged parents and spending time with our teenage daughters. Juggling all of these commitments, we often invariably face situations of pressure and stress.

## THE PROCESS

While a lot of us are good at making critical decisions in daily or predictable circumstances, that moment of crunch ultimately comes when one has to make life-or-death decisions under stress and massive pressure, and yet stay calm and perform at one's peak. To glean learnings from people who routinely operate in these trying circumstances, we created a Crisis Advisory Panel and spoke to a veteran airlines pilot, an ex-army commando and a distinguished senior police official – all working in some of the most difficult circumstances in India, and all of whom have rich learnings to share on being a 'rock under pressure'.

## THE LEARNINGS

1) Our enquiry into being calm in stressful situations began with learning the concept of gritflowness. (You can read more about this at www.thriveglobal.com/stories/the-secret-of-gritflowness). At the same time, our understanding from ancient wisdom reminded us that the mind has four functions: *manas* (sensing or experience), *chitta* (memory), *vivek* and *buddhi* (analysis and judgement), and *aham* (ego). Pressure is felt when you operate from any one function at a point in time. Thus, the interpretation of ancient learnings is that optimal performance under pressure takes place when one operates from *all* four functions, and with the absolute mindfulness of the Here and the Now.

   Athletes performing under pressure often speak of being 'in the zone', which means being one in mind and body. They allow for no difference between the mind, the body, or even different parts of the body; in fact, there is a sense of 'one-ment', where muscle memory kicks in through years of rigorous practice, till it has become unconscious mastery. The mind has learned to process the environment, physiology, competition – all within the skilful subconscious, resulting in absolute, perfect, complete alignment and 'flow', thereby leaving no space for any sense of pressure to seep in.

Another associated concept we learnt from our readings to help navigate 'the slings and arrows of outrageous fortune' is to build your own mental fortress. Simply put, reinforce your mind and make it strong with positive thoughts.

2) Eika and I were also inspired by a wonderful piece of wisdom shared by Yaw, an ex-Unilever colleague (from our Singapore days), and now one of the foremost business leaders in Africa. During a stressful period, I once shared the challenges I was facing dealing with the many metaphorical 'balls in the air' with Yaw. The latter asked me to take a deep breath and shared a powerful analogy: 'Imagine you are the ATC (Air Traffic Controller) tasked with landing multiple planes without mishap. The trick would be to focus on landing *one plane at a time*, while being aware of what is happening around you. But land one plane at a time.' The simple analogy worked its magic and has been stuck with us, helping both of us along our lives and careers. So, an enduring thank you to Yaw.
3) Finally, from detailed conversations with our Crisis Advisory Panel of professionals who operate routinely under pressure, we distilled down three further learnings as given below:

    a) **Prior Practice** for alternative scenarios helps immensely. When the heat of the battle is on or when crisis hits, you are in a better position as your muscle memory automatically comes to your aid. Hence the motto: Practice in times of peace and bleed less in war. All our crisis experts stressed on the importance of daily and repeated practice.

b) **Focussing on Breathing and Self-Talk** involves taking command of your breathing, which is a critical skill for being a rock under pressure. This practice helps tremendously since it forces you to concentrate on yourself, rather than the situation, and aids you in seeing the situation from a detached perspective.

c) **Take Advice You Can Trust** when in crisis. Speak to trusted others and be open to taking advice. Our crisis experts shared fascinating stories of advice given in critical situations. Sometimes, the driver of a police jeep or a cook from the army can give insights and viewpoints one might have missed.

While learnings in theory can only take us thus far, it is the applied use of our learnings in trying times that makes the difference. And so, we have been practicing the above-mentioned guidelines consciously on a daily basis so that it becomes a habit. We're happy to say, it has indeed helped us be a rock under pressure.

## RESOURCES

- *The Art of the Good Life: Clear Thinking for Business and a Better Life* by Rolf Dobelli
- *Anti Fragile: Things That Gain From Disorder* and *Fooled by Randomness: The Hidden Role of Chance in Life and in the Markets* by Nassim Nicholas Taleb

## TO THINK AND DO THIS WEEK

### THINK

What is your crisis coping mechanism? How do you deal with problems?

________________________________________

________________________________________

________________________________________

### DO

Meet people who deal with crises regularly: doctors, nurses, plumbers, electricians, traffic policemen, sportspeople, surgeons and more. Have a detailed discussion with them about how they deal with pressure.

________________________________________

________________________________________

________________________________________

Experience:

________________________________________

________________________________________

Learnings:

________________________________________

________________________________________

Challenges:

________________________________________

________________________________________

WEEK 9

# THE NEXT ORBIT OF LEADERSHIP

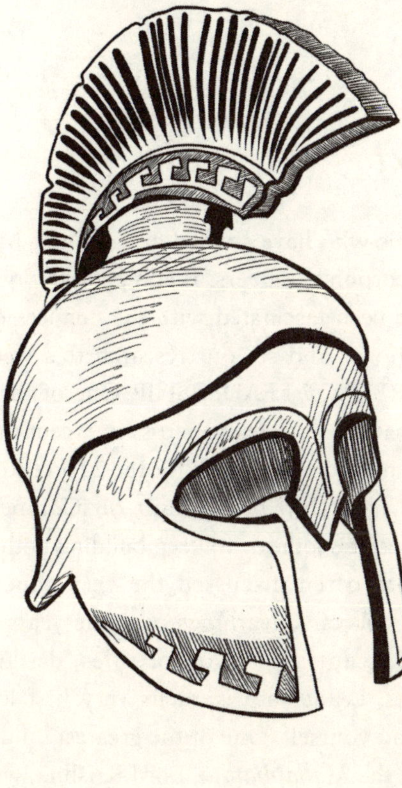

*'Leadership is an amazing disease.*
*It either cures you or kills you.'*

SOURAV GANGULY

## THE CONTEXT

As two people who have studied at a top-tier MBA school and built corporate careers at competitive organizations, Eika and I have been fascinated with the nuances of being in leadership positions. And so, our research this week was on THE NEXT ORBIT OF LEADERSHIP. One of the best talks on leadership that we have come across in recent times is that by General Norman Schwarzkopf's for the 21st century leaders. It was titled 'Leadership being Built on Competence and Character'. For us, the journey to keep building both continues.

We have both often discussed the very concept of the leader, and our collective learnings over the years have been that leadership is not a function of titles, designations or reporting armies. Leadership is, at its very first level, about being able to lead yourself. One of the greatest influencers and strategists from the *Mahabharata*, Lord Krishna, was a leader without any title whatsoever. He was neither the commander of an armed force, nor the post-war ruler-designate. In fact, he had even surrendered his armies to the enemy. And yet, he was the leader, thinker, and influencer behind the greatest epic war ever. Thus, leadership is first, foremost and most importantly, your conversation with your own self, long before there is external validation and recognition.

## THE PROCESS

As part of our attempt to decode leadership, we did three things: first, read *The Hero's Journey*, a classic by Joseph Campbell; had an animated debate on the process of becoming a leader; and attended lectures on the subject. We even spent time with a group of corporate leaders for their views and tips on leadership. Eika was fortunate to attend and hear Marshall Goldsmith, one of the world's best executive coaches, at the 2018 *Outlook* Business Summit; this came up just before her own session on 'Corporate Karma: Leadership Lessons from the Epics'. We had also attended a book launch of the *Catalyst* by Chandramouli Venkatesan, a veteran corporate leader.

Based on her years of experience, Eika has created her own model of leadership – The third S – Self Source Model. It is a three-step process that involves three levels of complexity, in ascending order. These are:

- Managing Situations/Business/Tasks/Projects: The first fluency level caters to task-based challenges all of us face at work, including managing multiple projects and lines of business. The reason this is classified as the first level of fluency is because managing of tasks/situations/business is potentially reducible to a checklist; long and complicated maybe, but still an itemized checklist to be checked off.
- Managing Stakeholders: The second fluency level involves the leader dealing with key stakeholders and sustaining relationships. This includes sharpening one's people insights

on motives and drivers, and managing interpersonal conflicts with greater ease. This fluency has greater complexity since the leader is also required to deal with irrationality and variance in people's behaviours, over and beyond task-based challenges and processes.

- Leading Self: At the third fluency level, leaders need to focus on their own Self, overcoming their fears and insecurities, and conquering their shadows. This level has the highest complexity because the leader has to not only deal with various tasks and account for the variability of others' behaviours, but also face their own anxieties and shortcomings. They must also take personal responsibility for emerging as their own biggest, brightest and most brilliant versions.

## THE LEARNINGS

1) The transition from the common man to a leader is one's own 'Hero's Journey' into their own Self. This comprises the path taken from one's homestead and business, through allies, shadows, mentors and tricksters (all stakeholders), to ordeals, conquests and resurrections (as the Self dons a leadership mantle) along the way. The most significant stage in this transition is the 'belly of the whale', that absolute silence wherein our leader's absolute focus and clarity is that of Self Awareness. Hence, if you want to be a successful leader, invest time and energy into interventions where you understand *yourself* first. As Swami Vivekananda famously said: 'You have to grow from the inside out.'
2) The journey from leader to visionary hero is one of establishing a higher purpose for the quest, the return with the elixir for the greater good. According to the *Bhagwad Gita*, the leader who is able to reach beyond their own Self

to align their team in resonance with a greater goal, within which the whole is greater than the sum of parts, is the eternal visionary. Similarly, as an effective leader, you will need followership. And people will consider you as a leader only if you can add value to their lives. So, focus on having a positive impact on people, by going beyond yourself.

3) Now that you have self-awareness, purpose and a positive impact, the next orbit of leadership is a function of your accelerated personal growth. And this transpires with clear vision and deliberate practice on a daily basis. Chandramouli spoke in detail about this principle in his book, *Catalyst,* with advice regarding converting time into experience and ensuring you to focus on the right set of learnings in the first half of your career to win in the second half of your career.

## RESOURCES

- *What Got You Here Won't Get You There: How Successful People Become Even More Successful!* by Marshall Goldsmith
- *Catalyst: The Ultimate Strategies on How to Win at Work and in Life* by Chandramouli Venkatesan
- The thoughts and writings of Naval Ravikant and Charlie Munger.
- *The Hero's Journey* by Joseph Campbell
- *Hit Refresh: The Quest to Rediscover Microsoft's Soul and Imagine a Better Future for Everyone* by Satya Nadella
- *The Secret of Leadership: Stories to Awaken, Inspire and Unleash the Leader Within* by Prakash Iyer

## TO THINK AND DO THIS WEEK

### THINK

Who are your heroes (real and fictional)? Why?

### DO

Draw your own hero's journey. Identify patterns. And draw into the future, too.

Experience:

Learnings:

Challenges:

WEEK 10

# POWER MORNINGS

*'In the morning a man walks with his whole body;*
*In the evening, only with his legs.'*

RALPH WALDO EMERSON

## THE CONTEXT

Eika is a pre-dawn riser, while I have perpetually struggled with waking up early, despite the obvious multiple benefits. Hence, our research area this week was on POWER MORNINGS, and looking for ways to increase our well being and effectiveness in the mornings. Robin Sharma's book, *The 5 AM Club*, stresses on the importance of waking up early and using the period of 5 a.m.–6 a.m. as a 'Victory Hour' for getting a daily head start on the meaningful goals in your life.

## THE PROCESS

To increase our knowledge on this subject, we scanned literature ranging from the Vedas to recent podcasts by an ex-Navy SEAL. We also spoke to a doctor on the 'dopamine hit' benefits of early morning routines, and set up an appointment with an ancient Yogi practitioner to understand more on the science of 'sun eating'.

We began by gaining an understanding of what ancient Indian wisdom says about the matter. While the Western concept of day is divided into 24 hours, the Puranic scriptures divide the day into eight divisions known as *prahar* – four for the day and four for the night. Interestingly, this is also how the classical Indian music ragas are organized, meant to activate a particular part or sense of the body at a particular time.

Here is the *prahar* clock, as interpreted from ancient texts by Eika:

*Prahars* of the Day:

1. **Purvanha** starts at the crack of dawn. This is the time for dynamism, increase in energy, patience and joy. The typical morning ragas related to this hour are Komala, Asawari, Todi, and Deshkara, among others.
2. **Madhyanha** starts from mid-day till the sun reaches it highest point of the day. This is the time for wisdom, knowledge, greater joy and success. The associated ragas are Shudhha Saranga, Ahir Lalita, and Gauda to name a few.
3. **Aparanha** marks the period known as afternoon; this is the quarter of the day when the sun journeys westward. This is the time for creativity, achievement and life. The associated ragas are Multani, Madhuvanti, and Bhimpalasi to name a few.
4. **Sayanha** commences post afternoon and lasts until sunset. This is the time for relaxation, coherence and joyfulness. The ragas typically played during this time are Mishra Pilu, Marwa, and Puriya Kalyana, among others.

*Prahars* of the Night:

5. **Pradosha** begins from the first quarter of the night, post-sunset. This is also the time for evening prayers and, therefore, a time for harmony, celebration and compassion. The ragas for this time of the night are Puriya, Rageshri, Desh, and Durga to name a few.
6. **Nishith** starts with the onset of darkness and emergence of the '*nishchari*' nocturnals. This is the body's time for restful sleep and peaceful slumber. Typically, the ragas associated with this time of the night are Darbari Kanhra, Malkaunsa, and Abhogi, among others.
7. **Triyama** represents the deepest hours of the night. This is the time for tranquillity, gentleness and serenity. Typical ragas played during this time are Sohini, Bhatiyara, and Nata Bhairava, among others.
8. **Usha** forms the quarter of the night that is pre-dawn. This is a time for heightened spiritual awareness, especially the Brahma Muhurta. This is the time for emotional strength, devotion and peace integration. The ragas associated with this time are Bhairavi, Bhairava, Ramakali, and Jogiya to name a few.

In addition to the *chakras* these ragas activate and heal, this science of the time and of the day is deeply associated with the food we eat, as well. In fact, Western science and medicine is slowly but surely beginning to understand and appreciate the relationship between the *prahars* and the circadian rhythms of the peak human behaviour and efficiency. We will be digging deeper into these interconnections as we go along our learning journey. For more details on which foods are suited to your mornings, noons and evenings, do spend time with a trusted dietician.

## THE LEARNINGS

1) The morning rituals in ancient wisdom – as part of the daily routine '*Dinacharya*' – are designed around bringing the body, mind and emotions into an aligned balance, fresh and ready for the day. They include the following step:
   - Wake up during the *Brahma Muhurta*, about an hour and a half before sunrise; this time is one of universal cosmic energy resonance.
   - Start the day with warm water, either with honey, lemon and ginger, or with cinnamon, black pepper and a dash of turmeric.
   - Splash your face with cold water and open the eyes. This balances the *doshas*. Gargle with one tablespoon of oil and rinse. Follow with a quick self-oil massage, ablutions and shower.
   - Now it is time for performing yoga to limber up and activate the body, followed by pranayama to align the *chakras* with one's breathing. End with meditation for conscious clarity.

   You are now activated, aligned and alive to face anything the day will offer you.

2) I have become a recent fan of the 4:30 a.m. club as proposed by ex-Navy SEAL Jocko Willink, and love his *Extreme Ownership* philosophy. (Also, check out his videos on YouTube for context). His hack for Power Mornings is thought-provoking. According to him, 'Don't think when you get up in the morning.' Get into your gym, run, yoga gear (kept out the night before) and go 'get some'. The temptation of checking your phone, making a to-do list or reading the news, hence, does not creep in and you start

your day pumped up. Try it. I have! It takes some doing, but works magically.

3) If you still need more motivation for Power Mornings, consider the Japanese concept of Ikigai. We were reading about it recently, and while some concepts are common sense and known to us (importance of routine, the need for a good breakfast and so on), the useful nugget to explore and interrogate was of Daily Purpose. The Ikigai concept says that waking up early and happy can be achieved if you build purpose to each day of your life, i.e. something meaningful that you will do each day (from creating something to helping somebody or meeting friends).

## RESOURCES

- *Extreme Ownership: How U.S. Navy SEALs Lead and Win* by Jocko Willink. Also check his podcasts and YouTube videos.
- *The 5 AM Club: Own Your Morning, Elevate Your Life* by Robin Sharma
- Investigate the numerous online essays on Ikigai.

## TO THINK AND DO THIS WEEK

### THINK

What is your favourite hour of the day and why?

### DO

Wake up at 5:30 a.m. this week and try to meditate, workout, read or write. Essentially, try any activity that is meaningful to you.

Experience:

Learnings:

Challenges:

**Use this table to record your daily discipline**

| Wake Up | 5 AM | 6 AM | 7 AM | 8 AM | Sleep Off | 9 PM | 10 PM | 11 PM | 12 AM |
|---|---|---|---|---|---|---|---|---|---|
| Day 1 | | | | | | | | | |
| Day 2 | | | | | | | | | |
| Day 3 | | | | | | | | | |
| Day 4 | | | | | | | | | |
| Day 5 | | | | | | | | | |
| Day 6 | | | | | | | | | |
| Day 7 | | | | | | | | | |

WEEK 11

# SPIRITUALITY AS A SUPERPOWER

*'You have to grow from the inside out.*
*None can teach you, none can make you spiritual.*
*There is no other teacher but your own soul.'*

SWAMI VIVEKANANDA

## THE CONTEXT

Is Elon Musk spiritual? Was Steve Jobs a follower of a spiritual group? What is spirituality? As Eika and I read stories of people who inspire us with their courage and fortitude through the ups and downs in their lives, we wanted to know more about their anchors: their spiritual lighthouse and their secret source of clarity. Which is why our research area this week was: SPIRITUALITY AS A SUPERPOWER.

## THE PROCESS

Eika continued her deep dive into the knowledge of the Vedas, while we also read up literature by thinkers like Deepak Chopra and Buddhist monk, Thich Nhat Hanh, who founded the Order of Interbeing. We also spent time with Brigadier Talwar, one of India's foremost oncologists and a fabulously spiritual human being (one can literally see his aura!). He spoke to us at length about his journey, and his videos were highly educational.

To begin with, we came to understand that spirituality, a much used and abused term, is actually the 'Science of the Spirit', much like physics is like a set of 'Laws of Matter and Energy' and biology is the 'Science of the Living'.

While there are multiple ways and philosophies (*darshans*) of understanding spirituality, one simple way, closest aligned to the concept of science, is the *Sankhya Darshan.* As per this strongly dualist philosophy, the universe is composed of two realities: *purusha* (masculine energy/creator) and *prakriti* (feminine divinity or matter/created). The joy of focussing on the energy, as well as on emotional and spiritual wellness takes care of intellectual and physical health and performance by itself. A *jiva* (living being) is that state in which the *purusha* is bonded to *prakriti* in some form.

While the *Sankhya* is the possible original inspiration for Einstein's relativity, as well as the basis for the wave–particle duality, what is even more interesting is the grounds that the philosophy lays for chemistry and the description of matter.

The *purusha* is the energy, the consciousness, and the life force that powers all existence.

The qualities of *prakriti* (matter), on the other hand, are introduced in the concept of the *gunas* (qualities). All *prakriti* has three *gunas*, but in different proportions. These are:

- Tamas: the quality of darkness, ignorance, lethargy, destruction and negativity.
- Rajas: the quality of activity, chaos, passion, and impulsivity.
- Sattva: the qualities of goodness, compassion, illumination, and positivity.

The interplay of these *gunas* defines the character of someone or something, as well as of nature, and hence, determines the progress of life.

The quest for spirituality, then, is the exploration of, union with and a deep dive into the *purusha*, the energy and life force that underlies and defines our very existence, and its liberation, beyond the matter that is our body. Spirituality allows us to access that oneness and resonance.

## THE LEARNINGS

1) Find your own God or belief system. You will need it once your immediate material goals are met to help you move from an acquisitive life to the one of fulfilment.
2) Spiritual path is no mumbo jumbo. The equation of Work x Worship = Wisdom is a life and career accelerator.
3) Spirituality enhances your inner essence (and fragrance). As such, life becomes effortless, and you feel blissful in every moment.

Spirituality is a path, process or a journey. It is a personal transformation. And so, we would encourage you to reflect on this and construct your own path.

### RESOURCES

- Immerse yourself in the writing of Swami Vivekananda
- Read the works of Deepak Chopra

## TO THINK AND DO THIS WEEK

### THINK

Who or what do you turn to when you're troubled, depressed, or feeling down and out? What does that do for you?

### DO

Make a vision board with your favourite inspirational quotes. real would be more fun than virtual; don't forget to include authors' names.

Experience:

Learnings:

Challenges:

WEEK 12

# GOING ORGANIC

*'Food commonly eaten for more than 150 years should be innocent until proven guilty, and food invented in the last 150 years is guilty until proven innocent.'*

MILES HASSELL

## THE CONTEXT

Our immediate provocation for this week's RedPill was a disturbing video that has been circulating on social media. It's about our poisoned food chain. In this era of fake news, and for our own health, we wanted to learn more on this. And so, our research area this week was about GOING ORGANIC, or at least getting a better understanding and control of our food supply system.

## THE PROCESS

This was not an easy topic. Big global lobbies have funded research and communication in this field, which has created multiple world-views. So, we met experts who have personally walked this path, and we immersed ourselves in their lives.

The learning journey has just begun, and we forge on (much beyond just this week) and grapple with questions such as abolishing processed sugar from our lives, overhauling our kitchens and throwing out all processed and packaged foods, and building organic farm supply chain linkages.

## THE LEARNINGS

1) This subject raises fabulous questions, the narratives for which are controlled tightly by food lobbies. The most basic is to question the source of your food. We once bought *methi* and *palak* from a big chain store; and these green, leafy vegetables, worryingly, ran colour when washed.

   Also, if rampant animal protein is linked to three of the most common killers in this age – diabetes, heart disease and cancer – surely it makes sense to question the food one is eating, from reconstituted milk and hormone-overloaded eggs, to preservative-laced packaged foods. Essentially, we need to be keenly aware of the food choices we're making.

As Eika's favourite swami, *vaid* and healer, Satya Prakash, says, 'Change your kitchen, and you will change your life.' According to him, our bodies and metabolism are perfectly adept at dealing with chemical colours, preservatives and adulterations, certainly up to a basic level of toxicity. However, what our physical body mechanisms haven't yet learnt to neutralize are hormonal influxes that get introduced through hormonally bred cattle that produce all our dairy and related products, or even growth-hormone bred poultry and meat produce. These kill our body's immunity, and also send our personal growth and maturity systems into an absolutely manic tizzy. Our antennae were certainly buzzing with all this new knowledge we gleaned.

2) We had an informative chat with Manisha Lath Gupta, a successful corporate professional and entrepreneur, who has made an amazing effort in going organic; to the extent of having a full-fledged ten-acre permaculture farm. (You can learn more about it on www.aanandaa.com). We were intrigued enough to read more on this subject, and chose two popular books on nutrition: *The China Study* by Colin and Thomas Campbell, and *The Obesity Code* by Dr Jason Fung.

   The major behaviourial change for us, however, involved reducing our intake of cooked foods (which, obviously, is not natural) and instead going big on fruit, and ensuring there was a constant and copious presence of organically grown fruit in the house, both for meals and snacking

3) Eika was immensely inspired by a visit to the weekly farmers market in Colaba (Mumbai). Over the week, she established a linkage with an urban farmer, a full-fledged corporate professional who, along with his two corporate friends, grows organic vegetables and fruits on a five-acre farm outside Mumbai; fortunately, he was happy to supply steady produce to us weekly. And so, we took our first few steps towards taking control of our food supply. Our suggestion is that you speak to people around you, as well. There is an emerging sub-culture of urban farmers (besides weekly farmers markets, as a temporary solution) one can tie up with and build a network of people who

can help you in this food cycle journey. In fact, inspired by the Maharashtra government's initiatives in organic and natural chemical-free agriculture, Eika has actually managed to set up a working group of *jaivik* experts, urban farmers, evangelists and advocates to create demand and market-linked organic produce supply chains.

## RESOURCES

- *The Omnivore's Dilemma: A Natural History of Four Meals* by Michael Pollan
- Join a local WhatsApp group run by an urban farmer.
- Find out more at www.TheFruitarian.com

## TO THINK AND DO THIS WEEK

### THINK

Can you name the foods, cosmetics and clothes (that you consume or use) for which you can establish value, source and supply chains?

### DO

Try going chemical free on some foods and cosmetics this week. Be careful to read food labels in the supermarket and avoid all artificial sources of food and drink. Hunt for chemical-free sources of your food, and try making or growing them at home.

Experience:

Learnings:

Challenges:

WEEK 13

# HACKING MARTIAL ARTS

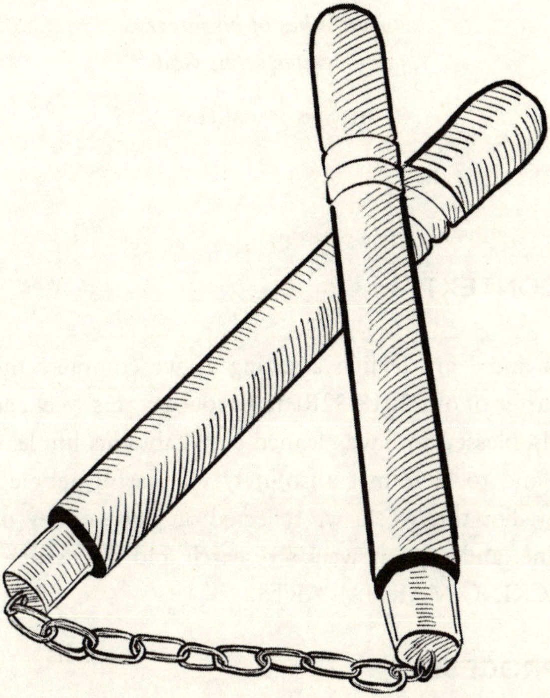

*'And how can a man die better*
*Than facing fearful odds*
*For the ashes of his father*
*And the temple of his Gods?'*

THOMAS MACAULEY

## THE CONTEXT

Eika and I are feeling amazing as we complete the first quarter of our 2018 52RedPills journey this week, and we are truly blessed to have gleaned such fabulous life learnings so far, and to have met absolutely wonderful people along the way. For this week, we reflected on our journey of self-discipline, and so, this week's research and discussions were on HACKING MARTIAL ARTS.

## THE PROCESS

Martial Arts are not just about fighting. For us, hacking martial arts is about raising our awareness, understanding our breathing, and gaining some basic survival skills. This RedPill is all about getting inspired by the principles of discipline and doing – two critical actions that can help build muscle memory. Most of our learning this week involved reflecting on and discussing the moves we have learnt in our practice of martial arts over the past few years.

## THE LEARNINGS

Eika and I would like to share some nuggets of our experience thus far from our practice of martial arts.

> Eika learnt the basics of Krav Maga, the famed Israeli martial art, seven years ago. Now, she teaches it's principles in her women safety workshops. These are principles one can apply in daily life to avoid 'intentional blindness' and be more aware of one's surroundings, especially in an unsafe world.

According to forensic data, coupled with insights from convicts, the learnings suggest that the one, and only one, difference between a soft and hard target is Awareness and Alertness. Criminals would any day choose an unaware, unmindful target over an aware person.

Being aware of your surroundings includes having no distractions. For instance, talking on the phone, listening to music via earphones, or being preoccupied with a loose *dupatta* or a fluttering scarf. Any one of these may mark you as an easy target. Hence, when in external or unsafe surroundings, act confident and be aware and focused.

Practice meditation every day to have a clear mind; this will also help you be aware. I have recently become a student of Shaolin Kung Fu, (under Shifu Kanishka Sharma's students), and it is fascinating the avenues of knowledge this opens up for the human mind.

There are three parts to this learning: *Chan* (Buddhist meditation), *Wu* (martial science) and *Yi* (medicine). In essence, this knowledge is about 'mastering yourself', which is built by daily discipline and meditation.

A couple of interesting points that stood out for me during this martial science training are:

- The best way to win a fight is to avoid it.
- Everyday items like pens and car keys, with simple training, can become devastating weapons in case of attack.
- An awareness of the human body, coupled with knowledge of physics (gravity and momentum), makes you appreciate yourself more.
- The mantra of self-defence, reiterated for us, was that if you are provoked and physically harassed, make sure that you are the first to hit hard and then run to safety.
- Both the martial arts stress on hitting an attacker on the face's five vulnerable points: the eyes, ears and nose.

## RESOURCES

- A host of online resources exist for an appreciation on Krav Maga.
- Discover the teachings of Shifu Kanishka Sharma on YouTube.

## TO THINK AND DO THIS WEEK

### THINK

How are you most likely to respond when physically threatened?

### DO

Drop in on a dojo, taekwondo or karate class in your neighbourhood. Sign up for a trial lesson and see if you would like to continue it.

Experience:

Learnings:

Challenges:

WEEK 14

# TURNING CURIOSITY INTO CREATIVITY

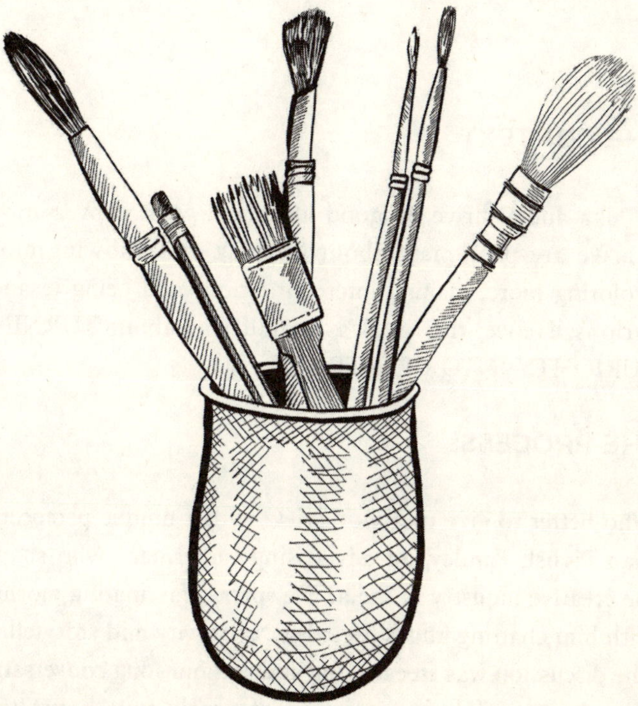

*'Creativity is intelligence having fun.'*

ALBERT EINSTEIN

## THE CONTEXT

Eika and I thrive on good ideas and great conversations. We are passionate about learning and knowing more, exploring more, making interconnections and being insanely curious. Hence, this week's RedPill was about TURNING CURIOSITY INTO CREATIVITY.

## THE PROCESS

Who better to give us a worldview with a unique perspective than Piyush Pandey, an advertising 'superman' who shaped the creative industry in India? We spent a fascinating morning with him chatting about life, ideas, creativity and storytelling. The discussion was free flowing and an hour-long conversation turned into a fabulous journey of nearly four hours (and might have continued had the legend not had to leave for a cricket match at Wankhede Stadium). While the day's chat with Piyush was not recorded and cannot be replicated *in toto*, we have listed below a few excerpts to capture an overall flavour about the subject of creativity.

## THE LEARNINGS

1) **Keep an open ear and a keen eye (no filters please).** There are no prescriptions for life and creativity. Passion and observation often become learning. Observation of life is critical. Appreciating life's many moments is key to absorbing learnings that can sometimes inspire lines, stories and scripts. That's how the magic in ad campaigns such as 'Chal Meri Luna' and SBI's 'Heera Kya Jaane' happened. According to Piyush, 'If you appreciate the idea, the idea will come back to you when you need it.' His story about the Cadbury brief, which he cracked on the flight back from San Francisco, is a fabulous example of this.

   **Piyush's advice:** 'Immerse yourself in the stories around you and file them away in your mind.'

2) **Build a network of sources of insights.** You can learn from anything and anywhere, every day. Stories are everywhere: with your driver, neighbours as you walk in the park, and with people on a train or a bus. Even with your local barber, who is a quintessential source of insights and nuggets, as per Piyush, *Nai baatunee hota hai* ('Barbers are very talkative'). And what happens, we asked him, when you run out of ideas? 'I study people,' was the answer. This includes especially two kinds of people: kids and old people, for the unadulterated truth. Kids are innocent and since old people can't care less, they say it as it is.

**Piyush's advice:** 'The more you interact with people who are not there under compulsion, constraints or civility, the better off you are with respect to learning.'

3) **Do not show or talk about the 'obvious'.**

Vodafone's casting of the chilled-out elderly couple Asha and Bala is a case in point, according to Piyush. Never shy away from asking questions in order to go beyond the obvious. Know that there are multiple emotions to be tapped into. Understand them well. For instance, know the difference between *hasya* and *vyang*.

Budget constraints can also sometimes be fabulous for creativity. The bioscope film for MP Tourism is a good example of this. The same principle, as we discussed, applies to raising kids. Do not give them every comfort. Make it a little difficult. Let them find creative solutions and hacks to their problems.

**Piyush's advice:** 'Seed your mind with the right thoughts. But to absorb this, you also need a sensitive mind. All this will enable inspirations for fresh creative thinking.'

## RESOURCES

- *Pandeymonium: Piyush Pandey On Advertising* by Piyush Pandey
- *Thinking, Fast and Slow* by Daniel Kahneman
- *Steal Like an Artist: 10 Things Nobody Told You About Being Creative* by Austin Kleon
- *Alchemy: The Dark Art and Curious Science of Creating Magic in Brands, Business, and Life* by Rory Sutherland
- *Lateral Thinking: Creativity Step by Step* by Edward de Bono
- *Originals: How Non-Conformists Move the World* by Adam Grant

## TO THINK AND DO THIS WEEK

### THINK

What was the funniest anecdote or who was the most entertaining person you remember from your childhood? Why?

### DO

Create something – skit, story, comic, jingle, ad, song or anything you like – and record it.

Experience:

Learnings:

Challenges:

WEEK 15

# FROM WHERE ON EARTH DO YOU DRAW YOUR ENERGY?

*'It is always the same with mountains.*
*Once you have lived with them for any length of time,*
*you belong to them.*
*There is no escape.'*

RUSKIN BOND*

## THE CONTEXT

This week's exercise was quite unusual. It was a travelling Red Pill, since we were both on the road. And as I was swamped with work, this topic originates more from Eika's worldview: FROM WHERE ON EARTH DO YOU DRAW YOUR ENERGY?

For Eika, it is, undoubtedly, the healing Himalayas. She goes there at least once a year and comes back with renewed energy every time.

---

* Ruskin Bond is our favourite author, whom we love to visit in Landour, a lovely stretch of paradise with an awe-inspiring view of the majestic Himalayas.

## THE PROCESS

Here is the foundation for her argument. The Himalayas, as we know, are young fold mountains. The Urals, the Appalachians and other European ranges were formed along with the cooling of the Earth, when land was first formed, and mountains were the 'wrinkles' in that landscape. The rocks and beliefs of these ranges are as old as the planet itself. The Himalayas however, were formed when the landmass of the Indian tectonic plate (of the Indo-Australian plate) collided with the Eurasian plate, around fifteen million years ago. As a result of the collision, the seabed was thrust upwards and became the land of the mountains. The Himalayas are, thus, unique in that they feature the salts, fossils and silt of the oceans, the flora and fauna of high lands, and soil from within the Earth.

This *panchtatva* (five elements) existence redefines the Himalayan Mountains' electromagnetic field and its chemical composition, lending them their charm, mystique, salt, spice, intrigue and comfort. And that is how the Himalayas became the soul in the sacred, the abode in ancient wisdom, and the hope in healing.

Legend has it that Adi Shankaracharya, the 8th century Indian philosopher, travelled all the way from Kerala to set up the *matthas* (monasteries) in the Himalayas. Numerous folklores, epics (including several stories from the *Mahabharata* and *Ramayana*) and multiple references in the scriptures make mention of these mountains, as well. According to one, when Lakshman was grievously wounded in the war with Ravana in Lanka, Hanuman was sent all the way to the Himalayas for the life-saving *sanjeevani booti*. Another story narrates Ravana's attempt to uproot Mount Kailash from the Himalayas and carry it all the way to Lanka.

The origin stories of River Ganga and all her tributaries – Bhagirathi, Alaknanda and Mandakini – are all linked to the majestic mountains, as well.

In more recent times, we know that many *tapasvis* and yogis venture into the Himalayas for *sanyaas* (renunciation), as they surrender to and gain transcendental wisdom of knowledge beyond the senses. Celebrities and respected personalities such as The Beatles, Steve Jobs, Barack Obama, Maharshi and Swami Sivananda have also visited these towering wonders.

## THE LEARNINGS

Hence, for Eika, the Himalayas is the *devabhumi* (the land of the Gods), and a place that must be visited twice a year. For me, on the other hand, it is the beaches and the *susagade* (laidback) feeling of Goa, with its sounds of the waves and seagulls, that provide a calming effect to my senses, enabling me to relax and get into a creative zone.

And so, the only key learning here is a question for you: from where on Earth do you draw your energy from? Our tip: discover it and go back to that place atleast once a year to replenish and re-energize.

### RESOURCES

- *Himalaya: Adventures, Meditation, Life* by Ruskin Bond and Namita Gokhale
- *The Rupa Book of Ruskin Bond's Himalayan Tales* by Ruskin Bond
- *A Book of Simple Living: Brief Notes from the Hills* by Ruskin Bond

## TO THINK AND DO THIS WEEK

### THINK

Identify what or where your 'happy space' is?

### DO

Create and lock down your plan within this quarter to soak in your 'happy space', whether it is long walks in lush, green environs, romping on a sandy beach or trekking in the mighty mountains.

Experience:

Learnings:

Challenges:

WEEK 16

# BOOST YOUR MEMORY POWER

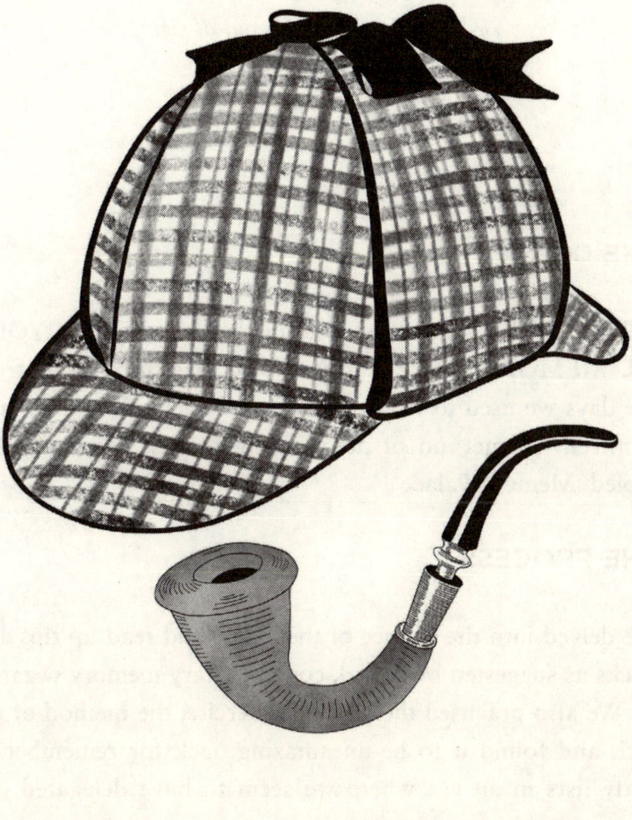

*'Memory is the power to revive again
in our minds those ideas
which after imprinting have disappeared,
or have been laid aside out of sight.'*

JOHN LOCKE

## THE CONTEXT

This week's immersion was on how to BOOST YOUR MEMORY POWER. This subject has inspired us from the days we used to read the stories of Sherlock Holmes and admired his method of memorizing things; especially, his fabled 'Memory Palace'.

## THE PROCESS

We delved into the science of the Vedas and read up tips and hacks as suggested by global, contemporary memory wizards.

We also practised the memory exercise, the method of the loci, and found it to be an amazing hack for remembering daily lists in an era where we seem to have delegated our memories to our smartphones.

## THE LEARNINGS

1) According to our ancient wisdom, out of the mind's four functions of the mind, *manas* denotes experiencing the world through your senses, while *chitta* is the memory. The data of your sensorial experiences (input from our five senses) gets processed through your intellectual analysis and judgement (*vivek* and *buddhi*) and through your ego and self (*aham*), before becoming hard coded as information in the *chitta*. The memory, thus, links back to a multipoint sensorial trigger, to be recalled and built upon when any or some of the linked sensorial triggers are activated. This means that if you involve all your senses in remembering something, you will be able to recollect it more efficiently.
2) Interestingly, there is also a process of this information or knowledge being further processed into wisdom or intuition, in the silence that is known as *rithambara*. Thus, when you hear (input) a song (data), your *chitta* (memory) may link it back to the smell of the rain when you heard that song earlier, or the visual of the hostel dorm where you heard it with your friends, or singing the song on a camp journey, or even the heartbreak of a lost love who dedicated the song to you, all in an instant recall of the various memory strands linked to the experiences related to that one song!
3) Repetition and rote, as we know from our school days, also cement data into memory. The oral learning and transmission of knowledge from teacher to student through hearing (*shruti*), and the student remembering it through repetitive memory (*smriti*); that is how the ancient scriptures, Vedas, Upanishads and the epics have been passed down from generation to generation over millennia. Hence, there is some logic to rote learning (colloquially

known as cramming). It, however, needs to be used for specific memory tasks, keenly leveraging the understanding of brain science.

4) Interestingly, a Brahmin's hair braid or *chotti* (the *shikha*) is linked to memory. The back of the head is the seat of *chitta*. And so, the gentle pulling, tying and massaging of the Brahmin student's *shikha* activates and sharpens his memory (*smriti*). It's amazing to consider how many of our ancient rituals are hard coded in scientific basis. As we explained in simple terms to our daughters, the *chotti* can be considered as an antenna that increases the mental concentration and boosts the memory power of a student.
5) We read and re-read two fascinating books on boosting memory (given below). Both bestselling authors are US memory champs and trainers of memory science. In essence, they talk about turning what you want to remember into a series of memorable visuals (the more outrageous the better, so that the visuals are vivid and sticky) pegged to something for easy retrieval.

The two most useful hacks for boosting your memory are the method of the loci and the peg method. The key to both is creative visualization and some practice; it works fabulously and can be learnt via practice in a week's time.

### RESOURCES

- *Moonwalking with Einstein: The Art and Science of Remembering Everything* by Joshua Foer
- *Instant Memory Training For Success: Practical Techniques for a Sharper Mind* by Chester Santos.

## TO THINK AND DO THIS WEEK

### THINK

How do you remember best: by using words, sounds, visuals, smells, associations and more?

### DO

Memorize your ten most frequently dialled mobile phone numbers. Try to remember your childhood home and mentally walk through all the rooms of your home to create your memory palace (reference Joshua Foer's book).

Also, challenge your memory cells by trying to do all your shopping from mental grocery lists.

Experience:

Learnings:

Challenges:

WEEK 17

# THE MAGICAL WORLD OF WHISKEY

*'Too much of anything is bad,*
*But too much good whiskey is barely enough.'*

MARK TWAIN

## THE CONTEXT

This week's RedPill was fundamentally different as it was more a learning via celebration; and the process certainly left us in high spirits as we explored the nuances, novelties and notes of THE MAGICAL WORLD OF WHISKEY.

This exploration also celebrated a decade of fabulous friendship with our friends, Shivam Misra and the legendary Indian designer, Anavila Sindhu Misra. And our whiskey exploration provided a great setting for this appreciation. While we have visited some of the finest whiskey estates in Scotland, this particular whiskey appreciation evening was experientially conducted via anecdotes and tasting right here at home.

## THE PROCESS

Shivam has worked as a senior corporate leader in the alcobev industry for the past two decades and knows his beverages. It was he who took us through a virtual journey of Scotland via his whiskey tour during the course of a lovely evening with our friends. We thank him for his massively detailed tasting notes!

## THE LEARNINGS

- We started with Oban 14 and Oban Little Bay. Both have a distinct citrus fruit nose. The 14, we found, has a bit of sea salt, while Little Bay has more than a hint of pepper on it. On the palate, both of them were fruity orange and citrus, even as peach and fig dance in between the flavours, drawing a bit of distinction between the two. They both have a long smooth finish true to the character of the distillery.
- We then moved to the Clynelish 14. This coastal highland malt has a distinct subtle floral opening nose and a yellow-gold appearance. Once it reached our palate, we enjoyed the light creamy citrus that comes through, along with a slight hint of honey. Its finish is slightly dry, subdued bitter and light brine. This makes it a classic coastal highland malt.
- It was then time for the big boys. The Lagavulin Double Matured enchanted us, especially the nose of this distiller's edition. Lagavulin is robust with the characteristic Lagavulin smoke that gets rounded off with raisin sweetness. Crispy malt with a hint of iodine! The palate is distinctively grassy to begin with, followed by a full peat as the smoke fills in. A slight tang of salt and then coffee and vanilla with a hint of fruit makes up the middle. Incredibly long finish with fruit, peat and oak.
- Then came the mother of all that we tasted: the Talisker 25 – one of the oldest single malt scotch whiskies made

by the sea on the shores of the Isle of Skye, a remote and ruggedly beautiful landscape in Scotland. The one that we tasted was filled in 1983 and bottled in 2008. Unreduced, a quiet nose, not hugely assertive, yet quite maritime (like a fresh ship's varnish). It had a faint nose prickle with a spicy briny, and distant smoke. The palate had a gentle start, immediately building in intensity. Slow and sweet, then building up with a peppery and hot kick, with significant balancing bitterness and salt, and a little smoke. Its finish was long and warm, which was slightly bitter and very dry. And while we were gingerly sipping, we could not miss the smokiness. At cask strength of 54.2 per cent ABV, it's incredible how wonderful this whiskey is on both the palate as well as the nose. A fitting finale to our evening wrapped up in memories.

## RESOURCES

- www.MasterOfMalt.com
- www.TheWhiskyExchange.com

## TO THINK AND DO THIS WEEK

### THINK

Which is your most favourite beverage and why?

### DO

Try a new beverage this week – a smoky single malt, a handmade gin or a local wine.

Experience:

Learnings:

Challenges:

WEEK 18

# ON LIFE HACKS

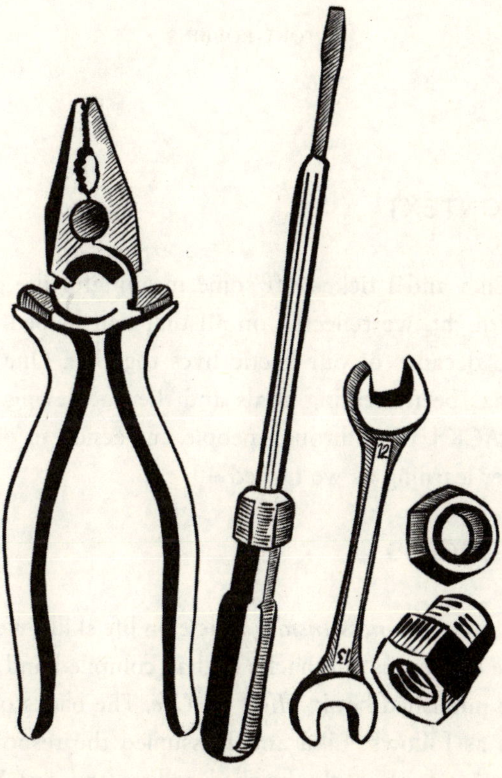

*'Goals are like magnets.*
*They'll attract the things that make them come true.'*

TONY ROBBINS

## THE CONTEXT

As Eika and I ticked off some meaningful life goals this fortnight, we reflected on all that had helped us in the last two decades of our hectic lives together. One constant theme has been creating goals and then achieving them via LIFE HACKS, be it through people immersion in our 30s or via hyper-learning as we turned 40.

## THE PROCESS

Inspired by a *Business Insider* article on life skills, we reflected on some of the tips and hacks we had compiled and shared in my first published book, *High on Life*. The backstory of this book is as follows: Eika and I assumed the responsibilities of adult life fairly early, finished college and our MBA, got married and had our first child, all by the age of 24. We both were also the older siblings in our respective households, the firstborns of our parents.

As such, we certainly do wish sometimes that we had someone older and wiser, personally and/or professionally, who would share his or her life tips and efficiency hacks, learnings and tricks with us. And that became our inspiration for *High on Life*, as we shared some of *our* early learnings.

## THE LEARNINGS

We'd like to share these quick hacks with young people starting out post-college, first jobbers and people in their late 20s.

1) Learn two things: how to type fast and the art of public speaking. This will help you save massive amounts of time and aid in your career and life always. (*See also RedPill on Effective Communication.*)
2) If you like meeting with and hosting people (Eika and I certainly do), take membership of a prestigious club in one of the smaller cities (non-metros) and use the reciprocal facility with the best clubs across metros, instead of waiting in line for decades for a Gymkhana kind of membership. New-age clubs like Soho House and Indus Club are very useful for professionals and entrepreneurs, too.
3) Be generous and give back. Most of us are extremely fortunate in life. Help deserving people with advice, time, little money if needed, contacts etc. One does not need to be a billionaire to start philanthropy. Also, our personal point of view is that giving back can be done in small steps and preferably without fuss and fanfare. (*See also RedPill on Philanthropy.*)

Though *High on Life* was written ten years ago, we were delighted to let three friends, who happen to be 'millennials' read and review it. We were super encouraged with their response and feedback, as it reiterated that the lessons and hacks are still relevant, even after a decade.

In summary, Eika and I are big believers in Time Leveraging. In essence, building a small set of meaningful actions and work streams; then building those actions over time, and leveraging the eighth wonder of the world, compounding, to deliver big results from those actions over time.

## RESOURCES

- *High on Life* by Siddharth Banerjee
- *Principles: Life and Work* by Ray Dalio
- *Give and Take: Why Helping Others Drives Our Success* by Adam Grant
- *The Code of the Extraordinary Mind: 10 Unconventional Laws to Redefine Your Life and Succeed on Your Own Terms* by Vishen Lakhiani

## TO THINK AND DO THIS WEEK

### THINK

Which life hacks have you discovered the hard way?

______________________________

______________________________

______________________________

### DO

Spend this week figuring out those tasks or activity that give you the maximum ROI (Return on Investment) for your time and effort. Try to analyze each task, activity and minute, and classify them as rocks, pebbles, sand or water (reference: YouTube video, 'A Valuable Lesson For A Happier Life'.)

______________________________

______________________________

______________________________

Experience:

______________________________

______________________________

Learnings:

______________________________

______________________________

Challenges:

______________________________

______________________________

WEEK 19

# BE A SUPER WOMAN

या देवी सर्वभूतेषु शक्ति-रूपेण संस्थिता।
नमस्तस्यै नमस्तस्यै नमस्तस्यै नमो नमः॥

*'To that devi who lives in all beings in the form of shakti, power, strength. Salutations to her, salutations, salutations again and again.'*

DURGA DEVI MANTRA

## THE CONTEXT

This week's RedPill – BE A SUPER WOMAN – is a constant learning journey for Eika and me, especially given that we have two teenage daughters to whom we want to pass on these lessons. Our conversation was catalysed by two events: a conference hosted by Facebook at their global headquarters in Menlo Park (San Francisco) where I attended a talk by the Facebook COO, Sheryl Sandberg; while Eika met eminent coach Marshall Goldsmith in Mumbai, where he spoke about his book, *How Women Rise*. In addition, we all saluted the superwomen in our lives on Mother's Day, which was celebrated in the week 19.

## THE PROCESS

This topic is obviously close to our hearts, as Eika attempts to finish writing her book (for the last four years), *Goddess in the Boardroom*, the Indian corporate woman leader's companion to Sheryl's book, *Lean In*. And so, we have been digging through ancient texts and modern-day research on issues like gender pay-gaps and board representation, as well as meeting women leaders in order to explore their life journeys for lessons and advice.

## THE LEARNINGS

1) Eika's starting premise is that it is much easier for women in India to break the so-called glass ceiling from a civilization perspective. Indeed, they have been doing so for centuries, whether as Goddesses Durga and Kaali in our mythology, or as queens in the last 300 years or as a prime minister in the past half a century. Basically, Indians do not have a problem with women in power or as leaders.

   What might need to be deeply considered and keenly debated in the current corporate world, nevertheless, is the reluctance among women to rise. The root cause behind this is a woman's innate nature and conditioning to live for others, and the worship of sacrifice as a virtue, given recent societal conditioning. However, when one balances the detractors in the current context with enablers, such as a supportive family and work ecosystems that addresses the 'guilt' factors, women leaders will blossom across industries in India. Many progressive organizations in India are already getting the mantra right on this, and Eika's assertion (and her life's work) is that Indian corporate women have an inherent advantage. And, thus, more women can rise to the top, sooner.

2) The discussion in the Marshall Goldsmith conference revolved around the assertion that women should rid themselves of their guilt. While women put their immediate current jobs ahead of their long-term careers and strive for perfection, the conversation in the room was about also looking at the big picture. One obvious suggestion from the discussion, as mercenary as it sounds, was that women leaders should learn to sell their skills, market themselves and speak for themselves, rather than just letting their work speak for itself.
3) For a woman to become 'super', she needs to shed the burden of societal expectations and dive into herself, wherein her 'social responsibilities' either get discarded from judgement or get embraced as her true nature. Thus, she builds her career only if that is what she really wants, versus building a career to earn 'merit' and social points.

### RESOURCES

- *Women Who Run with the Wolves: Myths and Stories of the Wild Woman Archetype* by Clarissa Pinkola
- *Lean In: Women, Work, and the Will to Lead* by Sheryl Sandberg
- *I Shouldn't Be Telling You This: How to Ask for the Money, Snag the Promotion, and Create the Career You Deserve* by Katie White

## TO THINK AND DO THIS WEEK

### THINK

Which women, real and fictional, do you find inspirational? Why?

### DO

For each day of this week, do one thing that makes you your own 'super person'.

Experience:

Learnings:

Challenges:

WEEK 20

# START A MOVEMENT

*'Get up, stand up. Stand up for your rights.*
*Get up, stand up. Don't give up the fight.'*

BOB MARLEY

## THE CONTEXT

The other day, I was listening to Jennifer Dulski (then Global Head of Groups and Community at Facebook) at their Menlo Park conference, and her words sparked off several thoughts, on what brings people together and what forms movements. Her signed book, which she gifted to us, holds powerful lessons within it, gleaned from her time at Yahoo, Google, Change.org and Facebook.

## THE PROCESS

We are already 20 weeks into '52Red Pills', and when Jennifer heard about our hyper-learning journey, she enthusiastically recommended that we bring alive the 52RedPills thought by establishing a Facebook Group that would host the 52RedPills Community and spark a movement. Inspired by her words and a subsequent discussion, this week's RedPill is START A

MOVEMENT. Let us begin with a question for each one of us: Have we, in our lives, ever started a movement?

## THE LEARNINGS

Based on our experiences, and the readings and conversations of the week, we have distilled three useful action points on sparking movements:

1) If you want to consider starting a movement, consider two Whys: WHY should you start (explains your passion) and WHY should others join in (explains the purpose)? We spoke about the time in 2009–10 that Eika had started a movement in Singapore called 'Beat the TV'; it was based on her passion for experiential learning for our kids (rather than digital screens). It became very popular amongst expat moms in Singapore due to shared concerns and, thus, a common purpose. We also recollected how some of us joined a movement and used our networks and group resources to become friends of GOONJ.
2) The second bucket of learning was about Fear and Inspiration. Sometimes, we do not start movements, even for causes that we deem worthy and relevant, because we believe that one voice can't make a difference. Yet, as Jennifer demonstrates in her book, there are several real cases of individuals who have used www.Change.org online petitions or Facebook groups and communities to spark off massive movements, inspire others and bring about real change.

   We also re-watched the famous TED Talk by famed entrepreneur Derek Sivers who talks about starting a movement. We suggest you to see it for both education and entertainment.

3) In today's interconnected digital world, where social networks can facilitate various movements, from the Arab Spring to the Ice Bucket Challenge, both individuals and organizations can utilize this power to solve issues – local or global – and make a positive difference. In fact, we join as many worthy movements as we can, from lending support to groups fighting against deforestation of urban green spaces, to friends who petition the government for better roads. We urge all our readers to support, if not start, movements that can help our community and the world.

Eika and I are certainly inspired to accelerate our respective movements.

Eika's purpose and passion has, over the last decade or so, been aligned to exploding and establishing ancient Indian wisdom on the global landscape. The mission is to establish India as the land of all answers, no matter what the questions. To fuel this, she created a worthy movement around this mission, be it through founding and curating events in this space, or through mobilizing community initiatives and evangelism through talks, panels and speeches.

Personally, there is one movement I support wholeheartedly and would for it to gain momentum, that of responsible driving on Indian roads, from making way for ambulances to helping lower the on-road accident incidences (amongst the highest in the world).

And anytime we have a doubt on the futility of one or few voices, we remember what former US President Barack Obama famously said: 'A change is brought about because ordinary people do extraordinary things.'

## RESOURCES

- Please read: 'How to Start a Movement', an article on https://m.huffpost.com/us/entry/12576552
- *Purposeful: Are You a Manager or a Movement Starter?* by Jennifer Dulski

## TO THINK AND DO THIS WEEK

THINK

Which causes are you most passionate about? What would you like to change in the world?

DO

Start a mini-movement this week on something that you'd like to champion in your building, office, society or neighbourhood. Whatever the cause, be the change.
Which causes are you most passionate about?

Experience:

Learnings:

Challenges:

P.S. We took our own advice and started a movement in our building to raise awareness about organic food possibilities for the residents and how we could help each other.

WEEK 21

# INSIDE A POLYMATH'S MIND

*'Simplicity is the ultimate sophistication.'*

ANON

## THE CONTEXT

This week's RedPill – INSIDE A POLYMATH'S MIND – is a topic close to heart since Eika and I are avid knowledge seekers trying to understand our world a bit better. In fact, two polymaths that we have grown up admiring are Leonardo da Vinci and Satyajit Ray.

## THE PROCESS

Of all the people we meet, some of our most fascinating conversations have been with people who can visualize the interconnections and multi-dimensional interactions in our world. Eika's favourite teacher in school was Ms Dayita Datta, India's first Mastermind and a bona fide polymath. My idol, however, is Sherlock Holmes, who, I would argue, is a polymath as he possessed the ability to see interconnections in his (chosen) areas of expertise.

In pursuit of a real-world polymath, we worked out a thought-provoking conversation this week with Sanjeev Sanyal, a veritable Renaissance man of the 21st century and a man of myriad accomplishments (Rhodes Scholar, Eisenhower Fellow, ex-Deutsche Bank global economist, Oxford University visiting faculty, bestselling author and currently the principal secretary at the Ministry of Finance, GOI). Further, to add more versatility to his bouquet of talents, he has just published his book of short stories (*Life over Two Beers and Other Stories*).

## THE LEARNINGS

1) Sanjeev spoke about the Complexity Theory, which forms the philosophical basis of his beliefs and choices. In this world, everything is interconnected; the individual parts are not important, the interactions are. An ant colony is a simple example of this. Hence, there are no silos, no ideal worlds or utopias. Masterplans and blueprints have massive drawbacks, and being a specialist is limiting. The polymath sees the world through the lens of Complex Adaptive Systems, and tries to deal with this complexity and evolve. Building on the above construct, the same principle of interconnected complexity and adaptivity applies to human learning as well.
2) The *Sankhya Darshan* in Indian philosophy also talks about the interwoven-ness of the universal fabric, with any and every operative system as its own complete form. So, you can either understand the human existence in its entirety and extrapolate the workings to decode the cosmos interplay, or vice versa. And so, the polymath simply allows

for the universal laws to play out and connect it all to his or her passions. And they have all spoken of their surrender to the laws of the Universe.

3) How does a polymath learn? Well, that's quite simple actually. By following a three-hack process:
    - Get the overall lay of the land using Google search and/or Wikipedia.
    - Gain understanding of key debates, terminologies, key characters and latest advances from whitepapers and publications on the Internet.
    - Speak to experts. Most are quite approachable, since they also want to learn more and test their hypotheses. And, if possible, create a community or a panel of people whose expertise you can trust and dip into. The secret is rigour of hard work to continuously build this knowledge, and then see or act on these interactions.

**Sanjeev's bonus tip on time management:** *Of all things to be done, only ONE thing should have a deadline. The rest should be done in due time, gradually and as fun. It was fun to start practicing this and we were able to see how relaxing it was as we balanced multiple plans and priorities.*

## RESOURCES

Check out these fascinating books by Sanjeev Sanyal:

- *The Indian Renaissance: India's Rise After a Thousand Years of Decline*
- *Land of the Seven Rivers: A Brief History of India's Geography*
- *The Ocean of Churn: How the Indian Ocean Shaped Human History*

## TO THINK AND DO THIS WEEK

### THINK

Which subjects most engaged your interest in your childhood?

___

___

___

### DO

This week, become an expert on a topic you know absolutely nothing about. Read up, research, meet experts, practice and prepare your own report on that subject. Collate it however you like it, in the form of videos, slides, photographs, audio recordings or a collage.

___

___

___

Experience:

___

___

Learnings:

___

___

Challenges:

___

___

WEEK 22

# BE (SUPER) INTERESTING

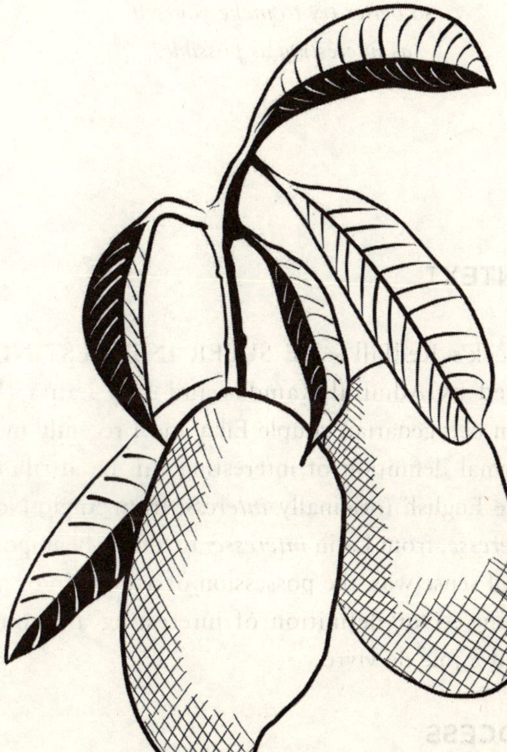

*'The person you will spend most time with*
*in your life is yourself,*
*so better try to make yourself*
*as interesting as possible.'*

ANON

## THE CONTEXT

This week's RedPill – BE SUPER INTERESTING – is inspired by Admiral Ramdas and Mrs Lalita (Lolly) Ramdas, an octogenarian couple Eika and I recently met.

The formal definition of interesting can be attributed to late Middle English (originally *interess*, from Anglo-Norman French *interesse*, from Latin *interesse*: to 'differ, be important'. The original sense was 'the possession of a share in or a right to something'. Our definition of interesting also plugs in passion and a joie de vivre.

## THE PROCESS

Simple. Meet interesting people. Have interesting conversations. Live an interesting life.

Our friend Dash loves cleaning other people's cupboards. As one can imagine, he gets all kinds of invitations! Another friend, Mangesh, has never drunk water in his life but famously imbibes all other kinds of liquids (including a daily diet of Diet Cokes), and has many stories to tell.

Our friend Sonali's mother earned her taekwondo black belt at the age of 54. And our above-mentioned octogenarian friends, Admiral Ramdas and Mrs Lolly Ramdas, constructed a farmhouse from scratch. They took a bald piece of land and planted 200 trees on it to transform it into a lush mango farm. They also became the 'lokpal' of AAP and a Greenpeace lead, respectively, and now they have started sending their organic farm produce across India.

## THE LEARNINGS

1) To be interesting to others, first be interesting to your own self. Cultivate your passion. Chase it like crazy. However random it may seem.

   For instance, one of Eika's dearest cousins, while being a senior IPS Officer, is also a PhD in History, and does the *Ramcharitamanas Adhyayan* in weekly editions.
2) Embrace your quirks. Let them be a part of you. Have fun with them.
3) Carry your creativity passionately through all your life. Nurture it and don't be limited by your age or stage of life to express it.

**Our challenge:** Become a storyteller of your favourite tales and anecdotes. Learn and absorb from anyone, anywhere and anything.

**Now think about this:** Who are the really interesting people you know?

**TIP:** You will be surprised how much you can learn about a person just by asking them to share a fun fact about themselves.

RESOURCES

- Read about the 'The Most Interesting Man in the World' advertising campaign online.
- Read the articles online from *Forbes* and *Bloomberg* on tips to be more interesting.

## TO THINK AND DO THIS WEEK

### THINK

What is that one super interesting thing (in a good way) about you the world does NOT know yet? How would you like them to find out?

### DO

Discover the super interesting stuff about five people you don't know so well. It could be people from your building or office, spouses of friends or even relatives.

Experience:

Learnings:

Challenges:

WEEK 23

# ON PHILANTHROPY

*'I would rather have it said, "He lived usefully", than, "He died rich".'*

BENJAMIN FRANKLIN

## THE CONTEXT

Do you know any corporate executive who would donate ₹ 1,850 crore of his own money to his company? Well, meeting one such amazing man got us started ON PHILANTHROPY, the RedPill for this week.

Dr V. A. Sastry, who donated the massive amount to Infosys, we read his full story in the *Economic Times*. Not surprising then that Mr Narayana Murthy, founder of Infosys, attended Dr Sastry's book *Unfiltered Me : A Life of Sense and Purpose* launch in mid 2018. Such is the respect and goodwill that the latter has earned from the Infosys folks.

## THE PROCESS

We debated the levels of philanthropy in our society versus the rest of the world, and we considered the subject through the lens of religion and culture.

In the Vedas, traditionally there are three kinds of 'giving':

1) *Daan*, donations made and largesse distributed upon wish fulfilment, or while conducting a yagya.
2) *Dakshina*, any fees or honorarium given to a cause, monastery, temple, spiritual guide or after a ritual. It is also the honorarium to a guru for education, training or guidance.
3) *Bhiksha*, is giving of alms or food to a begging mendicant in return for blessings.

None of these are prescriptive or mandatory. Rather, they are guidelines, sort of directive principles that incur *punya* or positive karma.

It is interesting to note how philanthropy is built into the Christian and the Islamic laws via the *tithe* (1/10th) and the *zakat* (1/3rd), respectively, of all material earnings and assets to be given away in charity. Hence, there are a plenitude of religious charitable foundations and religious organizations doing good work.

In the US, the pattern of philanthropy has changed from leaving a legacy mark on the world through trusts (Rockefeller, Ford, Carnegie et al.) to trying to channel massive funding to solve the most intractable and pressing problems facing mankind (Bill and Melinda Gates Foundation, Elon Musk, Larry Page et al.).

In fact, the Boy Scouts and Girl Scouts and Guides movement, so delightfully captured in the animated movie *Up*, actually trains young boys and girls on philanthropy and rewards them for kind and considerate behaviour. Our personal favourite is the concept of your 'good deed for the day', i.e. a small act of kindness and consideration to be performed every day, day after day.

Thus, the open debate we are currently into is what does it take to accelerate philanthropy in India?

Eika and I support the cause of 'Education of the Girl Child', and we get immense satisfaction from seeing how we can make a small difference by small acts of kindness.

## RESOURCES

- *Leaving Microsoft to Change the World: An Entrepreneur's Odyssey to Educate the World's Children* by John Wood
- *Giving: How Each of Us Can Change the World* by Bill Clinton
- TED Video: 'How capitalism and philanthropy can collaborate to solve big problems.'

## TO DO THIS WEEK

DO

Everybody has (or at least has heard of) To-Do lists. Do additionally consider To Help lists, which essentially are a small list of daily actions to help people, from writing a LinkedIn recommendation for a former team member, to connecting people with a trusted doctor, or sending a thoughtful gift to someone who might have helped you sometime in your life, and so on. This week, start by creating your own To Help list, consisting of ten actions to help others.

______________________________

______________________________

______________________________

______________________________

______________________________

______________________________

Experience:

______________________________

______________________________

Learnings:

______________________________

______________________________

Challenges:

______________________________

______________________________

WEEK 24

# INSIDE THE MINDS OF SPORTS CHAMPIONS

*'You just begin. You do the math.*
*You solve one problem.*
*And you solve the next problem.*
*And then the next.*
*And if you solve enough problems, you get to come home.'*

MARK WATNEY, *THE MARTIAN*

## THE CONTEXT

A meeting with MS Dhoni triggered this week's RedPill, as we got to reflect about being INSIDE THE MINDS OF SPORTS CHAMPIONS.

## THE PROCESS

Eika and I have been studying about the power of the mind from various perspectives. This week, I got a golden opportunity to speak to and listen a conversation with our celebrated cricket genius, MS Dhoni (MSD). 'Captain Cool', as he is popularly known, he has demonstrated his composed thought process time after time, especially under pressure.

## THE LEARNINGS

MSD's advice can be summarized as below:

1) Focus on the process, not on the results. The process is a result of hours and hours of deliberate practice, both individually and as a team, which prepares you for all kinds of situations. The process gets drilled into you and all you need to do is faithfully follow the process, especially when things are not going your way.
2) Getting distracted thinking about the results never ever helps.
3) Lastly, if you ever face unpredictable situations or challenges, use a combination of the process and your judgement to tide you through. The fighter in you always knows the right path. Have faith and follow it.

We also spoke to another global sport champion; this one, within our own family! Surbhi Misra was one of India's top women squash players and is now a successful sports entrepreneur in Jaipur. We asked her about her experiences and learnings on playing the sport at the highest levels and handling pressure.

Her top three tips and learnings were:

1) 'During pressure situations in matches, I tend to play the match in a point-by-point situation, and not worry about the outcome of the match.'
2) 'I take my time breathing well and being focussed on the present point. Self-talk and believing in myself has been the greatest help to me.'
3) 'The learning I have from these situations, which helps me even today is I never give up until the situation is over, just

like a match. Either it goes my way or the highway. Knock me down and I will get back stronger.'

One has to meet MSD and Surbhi to know how calm and unruffled they are. Some of it rubs off on you, as well.

We've spoken of performing under high-pressure situations earlier in this book, as well. And our conversations with MSD and Surbhi, and this is probably true given any high-stress, high-pressure or peak-performance context, bring out the truth and the wisdom behind the following *shloka* from the *Bhagwad Gita*:

कर्मण्येवाधिकारस्ते मा फलेषु कदाचन ।
मा कर्मफलहेतुर्भुर्मा ते संगोऽस्त्वकर्मणि ॥

'You have a right to perform your prescribed duty, but you are not entitled to the fruits of action. Never consider yourself to be the cause of the results of your activities, and never be attached to not doing your duty.'

– *Bhagavad Gita, Chapter II, Verse 47*

This, literally, absolutely and completely, is the mantra for success that we gleaned from this week's conversations. We have seen that when we have played point by point, ball by ball, step by step, in the here and the now, focussing on all that is within our own control (our own performance, our own response and our own karma), that is when we raise our chances of success.

## RESOURCES

- *It's Not About The Bike: My Journey Back to Life* by Lance Armstrong with Sally Jenkins
- *Open: An Autobiography* by Andre Agassi
- *The Greatest: My Own Story* by Muhammad Ali with Richard Durham

## TO THINK AND DO THIS WEEK

### THINK

Who are your top five favourite sports stars? Which are your five favourite sports, sports brands and sports songs?

___

___

___

### DO

It's Games Time! Play a new sport everyday this week for at least one hour. It can be anything – an outdoor team game, an indoor family game or even old games from your childhood. Go play your passion.

___

___

___

Experience:

___

___

Learnings:

___

___

Challenges:

___

___

WEEK 25

# ON GLOBETROTTING

*'I love to travel, but hate to arrive.'*

ALBERT EINSTEIN

## THE CONTEXT

Eika and I have been avid travellers all our lives, and since we want to explore more, this week's RedPill was ON GLOBETROTTING. Courtesy our two decades of corporate careers and our speaking engagements, we have visited six continents and 35 plus countries. Now, however, we have our sights set on more offbeat and novel travel experiences.

## THE PROCESS

This week, we spent time with a 'livewire' who has turned globetrotting into a fine art. Anindita Chatterjee is our typical millennial friend, who adroitly balances her CMO corporate role with her passion for global travel, and inspires us with her travel recommendations and her hacks for deals, bargains and experiences.

Anindita recently launched her travel site, www.travelchatter.in. Do check it out. And in case you read about her as a travel entrepreneur in the near future, remember you heard it first here!

## THE LEARNINGS

As Anindita finalizes the travel itinerary for her 65th country, here are some nuggets and tips from our detailed conversation with her that we plan to keep in mind when planning our next few countries to visit and enjoy:

1) What are Anindita's learnings and tips from ten years of planning global travel?
   a) First, make a list of your dream destinations, pen it down on a piece of paper, and put it up somewhere you can see from time to time. Only then will you work towards making that trip happen.
   b) Plan in advance. Get hold of your public holiday calendar and make a plan for the full year. Figure out which long weekends you can club along with some days off work, which will enable you to take off for a longer time. Have your holiday calendar ready at the start of the year.
   c) Never book travel packages from your own country. Read up about travel agents at your preferred destinations and book tours with them. They come at a much cheaper cost. At the end of the day, the local travel agents of your home country will also eventually get in touch with an agency in the country you want to visit and both will have their own margins, so you end up paying a lot more.

   She has a complete blog post with 20 hacks on this topic!

2) What does travel do for her? What lessons does she bring back into her life with all her globetrotting?

   Anindita strongly believes that her travels have made her a more fearless, open, adventurous, reflective and creative person, and that the word 'cannot' has been expunged from her dictionary. She has faced many difficult situations and figured out different ways and means to handle them, which has resulted in diverse, outstanding travel experiences. This insight gave us a hint as to why globetrotters do what they do and how it enriches them.

3) Her three favourite excursions, which she would recommended for our readers are:
   a) Romancing the silverback gorillas in Uganda.
   b) Dancing across a glacier in Argentina.
   c) Renting a scooty and driving 200 kms to see the majestic sunset at Cape St, Vincent, Sagres, also known as 'The End of the World', along the majestic Algarve coast in Portugal.

   PLUS, the most daring thing she has ever done? Travelled to Cyprus without a visa.

4) We also played a quick Rapid Fire Five Questions game on globetrotting:

   Q1) Top five favourite countries:

   A1) Iceland, Argentina, Jordan, Portugal and South Africa.

   Q2) A near-death experience:

   A2) Scuba diving in the rough seas in the Philippines. Also, the menacing stillness of the black surroundings of the Amazon forest at midnight, while sailing and looking for piranhas.

**Fun Fact:** *She possesses the jaw of the piranha she fished from the Amazon forest as a souvenir.*

Q3) Most impromptu trip:
A3) A recent New Year's plan to Ethiopia and Uganda.

Q4) India has not yet discovered:
A4) Jordan (It's a must do!).

Q5) Top tip for global travel:
A5) Always ask for help. People are always ready to help. The world is kinder and calmer than the media would have us think.

### RESOURCES

For more information and inspiration, check out Anindita's Travel Chatter website. She will be happy to help you plan your trips. Travel with her virtually on Instagram (@travel.chatter) and on Facebook (Travelchatter).

## TO THINK AND DO THIS WEEK

### THINK

Which exotic or far-flung fantasy destination did you visit in your childhood?

### DO

Collect, pull out, go through, and organize all your vacation photos from the last five years. Print them into albums, posters or collages. And plan your next quick holiday.

Experience:

Learnings:

Challenges:

WEEK 26

# GERMANY IS THE NEW ANCIENT INDIA

*'Indian philosophy insists that the sphere of logical thought is far exceeded by that of the mind's possible experiences of reality.'*

HEINRICH ZIMMER

## THE CONTEXT

At the halfway milestone of 52RedPills, we are making it awesome with a transcontinental RedPill, with me in Germany (courtesy of a business trip) and Eika in India. The provocation: GERMANY IS THE NEW ANCIENT INDIA!

**Note:** This topic was not in our original long list of RedPill subjects, but we have been deeply interested in it ever since we learnt that the folks who hunted most ferociously for the mythical land of Shambhala (Shangri La for some, akin to Dwarka in our mythology) were the Germans (especially Adolf Hitler and his handpicked reconnaissance squads).

## THE PROCESS

Eika has been studying the origin and spread of Sanskrit and yoga for the last few years. During this time, she zeroed in on many influences related to Germany, and we found multiple interesting commonalities. Meanwhile, I toured several places in Germany while I was there for a week and personally experienced how deeply they have embraced elements of our history and culture.

## THE LEARNINGS

1) Some of the greatest Sanskrit and Vedic scholars were German: Heinrich Zimmer and Karl Marx being two prominent ones. Zimmer was also an immense fan of Adi Shankaracharya. From the swastika symbol and the concept of the Aryan Race, to Buddhist teachings (*Siddhartha* by German author Herman Hesse is a classic), Germany has gained much intellectual stimulus from the Vedas and the philosophies of ancient India.
2) It was surprising to learn that there are more schools of Sanskrit in Germany than there are in India. Also, Germany also offers many well-regarded homeopathy and Ayurveda courses and higher-study programmes. We plan to find out what uses of this ancient language and medicine system has Germany been able to harness, from which India could well benefit.
3) According to a paper we read, a professor at the University of Heidelberg claims that the majority of Sanskrit scholars around the world, including those at the Harvard and UC Berkeley Universities in the US, and the Oxford and Edinburgh in UK, are Germans.* Some are working on

* Ghosh, Aditya. 'EXCLUSIVE: Germans to Be the Eventual Custodians of Sanskrit?' India Today, April 15, 2015. https://www.indiatoday.in/india/story/germany-sanskrit-applications-university-248605-2015-04-15.

deciphering the Vedas and Upanishads, while others are looking at how Sanskrit can help develop a simplified, hence more universal and powerful computing language. Are we, as Indians, paying attention to this and leveraging our own gifts?

Eika and I debated about the possibilities of a German and Indian mega-alliance, which would provide a new global order for arts, culture and philosophy. After all the talk on US and China, now this is an alliance that would be very interesting to visualize!

**Net Summary:** A trip to Germany would be an interesting experience for all those who want to see the deep immersion into Sanskrit and yoga in a foreign country.

## RESOURCES

- *History of Western Philosophy* by Bertrand Russell
- *Philosophies of India* by Heinrich Zimmer
- *Shambhala: In Search of the New Era* by Nicholas Roerich
- Useful link: 'German Search for Indian Roots', an article by M. Rajivlochan
- Also check: www.tribuneindia.com/2004/20041219/spectrum/book4.htm

## TO THINK AND DO THIS WEEK

### THINK

Which civilization fascinates you the most? Why? What would you like to know about it?

_______________

_______________

_______________

### DO

Explore one country on each continent each day this week. Research its common linkages and roots to your own country, as well as the many aspects of its civilization (cultural, historic, economic, social etc.).

_______________

_______________

_______________

Experience:

_______________

_______________

Learnings:

_______________

_______________

Challenges:

_______________

_______________

WEEK 27

# RUNNING AS A PASSION

*'The point is whether or not I improved over yesterday. In long-distance running the only opponent you have to beat is yourself, the way you used to be.'*

HARUKI MURAKAMI

## THE CONTEXT

I have been passionate about running for the past one decade, so a calf injury provided the backdrop for this week's topic of RUNNING AS A PASSION. According to a statistic by a veteran long-distance training coach, 63 per cent of long-distance runners end up injuring themselves, hence, the need to reflect and refresh the dos and don'ts of running.

## THE PROCESS

We discussed one of the best books on life and long-distance running that we had come across – Haruki Murakami's *What I Talk About When I Talk About Running* – and several of its insightful lessons.

We also reflected on the five key principles that we have absorbed from three friends who share this fabulous passion for running: Ash Nath, one of India's foremost marathoners; Shibani Gharat, famed journalist by profession and fantastic long-distance runner by passion; and finally my occasional running partner, Avinash Pant, a senior corporate leader and, more importantly, the most passionate sportsman that one could find in the business world.

## THE LEARNINGS

1) **Learn the Basics:** The human body is capable of immense feats, but one needs to progress gradually, incrementally increasing the stress load with periodic rest phases. I started running about 11 years ago when I was on an international posting in Singapore. I began with running 5 kilometres, then gradually increased to 10 kilometres, and finally went on to run a few half-marathons in a year. Ash Nath's Running Skills Workshops are a great way to understand your body and your running techniques.
2) **Build Capacity:** You need this to get stronger. Only then introduce intensity and speed. Regular interval training helps.
3) **Build Stamina:** Increase your run distance gradually. Since running is an impact sport, one has to be careful in terms of increasing mileage too abruptly. There is a general rule of thumb of about 10 per cent every week with a pull back every fourth week. And of course, listen to your body for signs of overuse injury.
4) **Add Variations to Build Strength:** Think of your (desired) running body as a sports car. After a certain number of laps around the racing track, the car needs to go into a pit stop for repairs and renewal. A runner also needs to complement his cardio or runs with strength, flexibility and

balance. A regular gym and yoga regimen is of great help to long-distance runners.

5) **Avoid Injury:** Avoid ITB (ilotibial band) tightness. This band runs along the outside of the thigh from the hip to the knee, and it's an area that runners have a high possibility of injuring. Using a foam roller to stretch this part (lie on the roller on your side and roll over the whole area) can help prevent injuries to the ITB. Another curiously bothersome area that only presents itself in longer distance running is chafing, which includes nipple bleeding or soreness or blisters on the toes. The best solution is to apply Vaseline or 'body glide' to nipples and toes, and of course, use good quality wicking socks and running tops. Finally, shoe selection is critical, something that is different from runner to runner. Some runners prefer cushioned shoes (Air Nikes and Under Armour), while others prefer to be as minimalistic as possible (Vibram is a good choice).

In summary, there is a Zen-like happiness to long-distance running that can only be felt, not described. To me, the best runners' high is experienced on the longer runs. Here's to running long and running injury free! As Murakami says in his book: 'Pain is inevitable. Suffering is optional.'

RESOURCES

- www.redbull.com/gb-en/ten-tips-for-long-distance-running
- www.runtastic.com

WEEK 28

# DECLUTTER YOUR LIFE

*'Tidying your physical space allows you to tend to your psychological space.'*

MARIE KUNDO

## THE CONTEXT

We accumulate many material possessions in our lives. And so far, Eika and I have led our lives on the move – from India to Singapore, to India to Sri Lanka and back to India. So, spring-cleaning sort of naturally happened. However, in the last three years, we have been stable and fixed in one city, and we have added more material things than we would have liked. Hence, this week, Eika and I were determined to learn some secrets to get back our lives and our possessions to the sweet and simple. DECLUTTER YOUR LIFE was our RedPill of exploration this week.

## THE PROCESS

The ancient texts that Eika read indicated that clutter, material or otherwise, allows in stagnancy and ennui, attracting sickness and disease. Whereas decluttering allows for flow and movement, true for the body, mind and spirit, and also for our evolution. In fact, the *Bhagwad Gita* speaks of *kshetra* or territory or property and of *kshetragna* or owner or proprietor, and how one can maintain and keep one's physical space, as well as one's own self clean. We combined these discussions by learning from the modern-day expertise and writings of the global phenomenon in this space, Marie Kundo.

## THE LEARNINGS

1) **Declutter Your Body:** There are multiple theories around decluttering one's body. We can detox our bodies by various cleansing rituals. A popular ancient practice is *Shankh Prakshalan*, a yogic detox with warm salted water. Other detox rituals involve green juices, kale and spinach, carrot, beetroot and ginger, and so on. Finally, one can explore intermittent fasting, with the right balance. In fact, Eika and I tried it this week (albeit with a slow start) and we could immediately feel the difference in our energy levels.

2) **Declutter Your Mind:** It is common to declutter one's mind by putting our thoughts or activities down on paper or online in the form of to-do lists, planners, calendars. But one of the best methods is the 3D Principle: Do, Delete and Delegate. If our work is done efficiently, our response times are faster, and our teams have the opportunity to grow via our delegation. We both use excel sheets and sticky notes for our to-do lists and our weekly planning lists extensively. And we find great utility in ensuring that we share our lists with our support system at home (maids) and at work (our executive assistants).

3) **Declutter Your Physical Space:** One can declutter one's physical spaces (office, desk, home, cupboard and wardrobe) to help with clarity of thought. One of our friends shifts into a one-bedroom apartment for five–six months every three years, just to force himself to strip down to bare basics and declutter his life completely. *Fly Lady* Marla Cilley recommends the practice of removing 27 physical items from your space every day, using the principle of Remove, Recycle (even donate) and Repurpose. Similarly, Kon Mari, a Japanese method by Marie Kondo, is a super-interesting way to approach decluttering as a fine art! On a lighter note, we tried the Marie Kondo method for this week but stopped after Eika threw out moth-eaten travel magazines that I had collected from a decade back!

4) **Declutter Your Spirit:** Now, here is the ultimate declutter task. Nirvana, moksha or salvation is achieved only when there is absolute decluttering of all spaces – physical or *manas* (*sthula sharira,* gross body), intellectual and emotional or *buddhi* and *chitta* (*sukshma sharira,* subtle body) and the spirit and soul or *atma*. The ultimate declutter is about shedding off even your energy or karmic impressions, which means repaying and settling of all karmic debts to then attain nirvana and become one with the stream of consciousness in the Absolute.

   **Note:** You might want to get to this last of all.

As Marie Kundo says, 'Tidying is the act of confronting yourself.'

## RESOURCES

- *The Life-Changing Magic Of Tidying* by Marie Kundo
- *Sink Reflections: Overwhelmed? Disorganized? Living in Chaos? Discover the Secrets That Have Changed the Lives of More Than Half a Million Families* by Marla Cilley
- *The Sentimental Person's Guide to Decluttering* by Claire Middleton
- *The Checklist Manifesto: How to Get Things Right* by Atul Gawande

## TO THINK AND DO THIS WEEK

THINK

How do you personally declutter your mind and emotions?

________________________________________

________________________________________

________________________________________

DO

Discard five items, every day this week. You'd be surprised at how much you can throw away, even from your bathroom and shoe cupboards. Decluttering old newspapers and magazines also counts. Don't be surprised if you get addicted to this.

________________________________________

________________________________________

________________________________________

Experience:

________________________________________

________________________________________

Learnings:

________________________________________

________________________________________

Challenges:

________________________________________

________________________________________

WEEK 29

# GRATITUDE IS AN ATTITUDE

*'Gratitude turns what we have into enough, and more.'*

ANON

## THE CONTEXT

This week's RedPill, GRATITUDE IS AN ATTITUDE, is a set of learnings and conversations we had with our daughters all week. What is interesting is that the catalyst for this topic came through some insightful conversations with our dear friends, Divya Palat and Aditya Hitkari. A big thank you to both for sharing their thoughts and stories created across their life journeys.

## THE LEARNINGS

Since this topic is deeply personal, there were no set process or prescriptions we followed. Below are just three thoughts we practice into our daily lives:

1) It is extremely important to appreciate that an intricate web woven by the effort and consideration of countless people is what supports our lives. The unseen daily exertions of others are behind each of the innumerable elements that

sustain and enhance our daily existence, from the food we eat to the products and amenities we use. Moment by moment, the natural environment supports and makes our lives possible. Gratitude is, thus, the joyful recognition of support. So, take a moment out and thank the driver, maid, liftman, the tea server and others. Remember: it is not for them only, you are following a cosmic law of gratitude.

2) Gratitude has also been defined and quantified in ancient Indian texts as the three debts or the *rnatraya* in the *Taittriya Samhita*. These are debts we are born with, accrue and repay during our lifetimes, as described below:

***Deva-Rna***: Our debts to our gods and the universe. Repaid through *yagnas* (sacrifices) and living in harmony with nature.

***Pitr-Rna***: Our debts to our parents and ancestors. Repaid by raising our children to be good citizens and better human beings.

***Rishi-Rna***: The debts we owe to our teachers and gurus. Repaid by honouring our education, and being an ever-learner.

And then there is the larger universal debt to the nation, the ***Rashtra-Rna***; and our debt to humanity and gratitude for our human birth, the ***Manusya-Rna***.

It is only when one fulfils all these debts and repays the *rna*s that one fulfils their human birth.

And when the balance of human behaviour is destroyed through mindless violence and violation of basic human values, then, as the *Bhagwad Gita* says:

*Yada yada hi dharmasya;*
*Glanir bhavati bharataha;*
*Abhyutthanam adharmasya;*
*Tadatmanam srjamy aham*

'The Universe responds with its own consequences and manifestations and avatars. So, stay true and dutiful, stay in humility and gratitude, stay in respect and humanity. Stay human.'

Different practices and religions have evolved different ways of expressing gratitude. From festivals (Thanksgiving and Shraddh) to the prayers offered to the Lord before every meal, the *naivaidyam* in every ritual and rite, and the bowing of head and folding of hands; all of which signify the submission and surrender to the Absolute for the privilege of life and love. So, take a moment to send out a daily thank you to the universe for the food, family, health and job you enjoy). Express gratitude for what you have.

3) Lastly, gratitude is not reserved for just bad times. Often, we become grateful in times of crises. Instead, gratitude should be a regular and daily practice. As Saint Kabir said: *Dukh mein simran sab karein, sukh mein kare na koi. Jo sukh mein simran kare, dukh kahe ko hoye.*

The above learnings have inspired us to maintain a Gratitude Journal, within which we pen down all the small and big things that we have gratitude for in our daily lives.

## RESOURCES

- *The Secret* by Rhonda Bryne
- *Eat, Pray, Love* by Elizabeth Gilbert
- For more in-depth understanding on this subject, read the teachings of the 13th Century Buddhist priest, Nichiren.

## TO THINK AND DO THIS WEEK

### THINK

How, when and what is your way of expressing gratitude for the small and big things, from fuel in your car to good health and wealth?

________________________________________

________________________________________

________________________________________

### DO

Start and maintain a Gratitude Journal this week. Write down three specific things, people and events you are grateful for that day. Be warned, this might become a happy habit.

________________________________________

________________________________________

________________________________________

Experience:

________________________________________

________________________________________

Learnings:

________________________________________

________________________________________

Challenges:

________________________________________

________________________________________

WEEK 30

# THE REAL SOCIAL NETWORK

*'The bond that links your true family is not one of blood,*
*but of respect and joy in each other's life.*
*Rarely do members of one family grow up under the same roof.'*

RICHARD BACH

## THE CONTEXT

This week's RedPill, THE REAL SOCIAL NETWORK was prompted by a lovely gathering of friends in Kuala Lumpur for a 'Big 40' birthday bash, and our friend Sumiti Tandon's belief that this is the 'ultimate' RedPill for happiness and joy in life.

## THE PROCESS

The original provocation for this enquiry came from a Raptitude.com essay we read called, 'How to Slow Down Time', which speaks about social relationships being linked to personal happiness – a useful reminder for all of us.

One of our dear friends, Aparajita Bharti, pointed us to the fascinating intergenerational Harvard study, 'Good Genes are Nice, but Joy is Better', and we immersed ourselves in the same. We also got engrossed in the Robert Waldinger TED video (by the same name) with results of the study spanning across 80 years on human happiness and health, which concludes that nothing else matters as much as meaningful relationships when it comes to 'happiness'.

## THE LEARNINGS

1) There is substantial research from Japan that emphasizes how deep friendships and meaningful social relationships are a critical factor for a successful and happy life. Hence, invest time, energy, effort and emotion into relationships, but always remember, quality over quantity.
2) Eika and I have been expatriates across Singapore and Sri Lanka, and we have closely experienced 'friends-who-become-family'. We are grateful for our friendships that have been mutually nourished and evolved over the years. The key is to develop ways to stay connected and not lose touch.

   A fabulous way we have found is an annual family update email that goes out to friends separated by geography. A classic inspiration for us has been 'The Gill Bulletin' (an annual family newsletter courtesy Kuldip and Tari, our lovely couple friends from Singapore)
3) Scientific research backs this up from an evolutionary perspective, as well. A Stanford University article concluded that 'social connectivity is key to our survival' due to the release of the oxytocin hormone, which meaningful social relationships can provide, and, perhaps, virtual platforms cannot help with. Hence, the need for phone calls and in-person meets, rather than texts and messages. For instance, while Eika and I get countless birthday wishes on social

media and phone calls, what really makes the day special is an effort in terms of an in-person catch-up or a handmade card.

Nandini told us an interesting factoid: While we might like to believe that intimate, deeply emotional social relationships are the purview of human beings alone, and maybe grudgingly even condescend to extend emotional bonds to animals, the fact is that even trees and shrubs and other vegetation runs its own network called the Rhizome Network, also commonly known as the wood wide web.

This network consists of the entire underground ecosystem: roots, bacteria, soil nodes and even worms and other underground insects. This is a very alive, vibrant and fertile network of communication and nutrition, among other exchanges. When there's a fire or a threat in one part of the forest, the other end is made aware of the same, which then responds by exuding greater sap, thus, making the trunk and branches damper and wetter, and, thereby, more difficult to burn. Some trees are even known to dump all their nutrition into the rhizome network before dying so that their nutrients are made available to the rest of the network before their roots dry up.

And we thought only human beings were evolved! And that only *we* had the emotional and intellectual capabilities or desires to create strong emotional and social support groups and 'hangout' buddies.

## RESOURCES

- *Dil Chahta Hai* and *Zindagi Milegi Na Dobara*, two movies that may facilitate oxytocin release.
- *The Perks of Being a Wallflower* by Stephen Chbosky
- The works of Robert Waldinger.

## TO THINK AND DO THIS WEEK

### THINK

What would your findings be if you were to conduct an audit of all your social media and networks? Of time spent, of people you know offline as well, and the value it or they add to your life?

### DO

Each day of this week, call at least one person close to you that you haven't spoken to in one year – old school friends, teachers, cousins and relatives. Increase your joy and, possibly, your lifespan in the process.

Experience:

Learnings:

Challenges:

WEEK 31

# THE SCIENCE OF INDIAN ASTROLOGY

*'There is a tide in the affairs of men.*
*Which taken at the flood, leads on to fortune;*
*Omitted, all the voyage of their life*
*Is bound in shallows and in miseries.*
*On such a full sea are we now afloat.*
*And we must take the current when it serves,*
*Or lose our ventures.'*

BRUTUS IN *JULIUS CAESAR*, WILLIAM SHAKESPEARE

## THE CONTEXT

We have wanted to do this week's RedPill – THE SCIENCE OF INDIAN ASTROLOGY – for long! The compelling reason for understanding this discipline is the debate that Eika and I have often had about whether we create our destiny with our actions or is it that everything is preordained, and we are merely players on the stage of life (with a hat-tip to William Shakespeare).

## THE PROCESS

Astrology is a fascinating area because of its interdisciplinary nature, combining astronomy, physics, math, chemistry, biology and psychology. This gave us a valid reason to understand it rather than dismiss it as hocus-pocus and superstition-based. We spent time researching how astrology travelled from ancient Greece to India and how the *rishi*s (seers) of ancient Indian had worked out the Earth's wobble and tilt ratio much before sophisticated NASA tools came into play! We read up on Parashara, the father of Indian astrology; the contributions of other Indian thinkers such as Aryabhatta, Yajnavalkya, Lagadha, Bhaskar, Garga and Brighu; and studied the history of Ujjain, which was the centre of Indian astrology for many millennia.

We also spent some fabulous hours with three astrology experts, one of whom has devised a two-decades-of-research powered astrology software to understand and explain how planets play a (definitive) part in human lives.

In essence, our astrology experts were unequivocal in stating that the planetary positions have already determined one's life. Now this took me time to soak in since I have strong confidence in my own efforts and, hence, a strong belief that I shape my own destiny.

It was also interesting to learn some truly amazing facts. Did you know that Amitabh Bachchan, Jeetendra and Rajesh Khanna – all the superstars of Bollywood cinema in the 1970–80s – share the same birth year (1942)? Similarly, the superstars of the 1990s–2000s, Shahrukh Khan, Aamir and Salman were all born in 1965. In fact, two of our experts had accurately predicted (and published) the outcome of several complex events, months before they happened.

So if our destinies and life-scripts are already pre-decided, what were our learnings?

## THE LEARNINGS

1) Indian Astrology uses a more rigorous methodology (with focus on the Sun, Mercury and the Moon) than the Western system. We discovered this week that our Sun signs are incorrect, if we go by the Indian system.

   **Note:** Linda Goodman, who also came to India and learnt some aspects of Indian astrology, uses Western sun signs.

   You all may want to check your sun signs, based on the Indian system by feeding in three details – date, time and place of birth – and then consulting an expert. This will give you an overall script of your life, and your karmic quota. How much you believe in it and the associated concepts of karma is a different debate altogether.

2) I kept asking the question, if the stars and planets govern one's life-script, what is the role of human endeavour? Why should we struggle with fate? We discussed two practical cases: Astrology can predict our areas of strength. So, if one knows what one can be good at, they don't waste time and energy fighting destiny and trying to figure it out organically and through trial-and-error. Like bankers who become authors or professionals who become bakers and painters. Secondly, astrology can come in useful at crucial crossroads of life, when it can give cues to next steps, possible paths and options.

3) Many of us working in formal organizations have been exposed to psychometric tools like MBTI (Myer Briggs Type Indicator). It is interesting that a simple

combination of Sun, Mercury and the Moon-based individual kaleidoscopes can help in understanding human dynamics and transactional analysis (dealing with your team, managing your boss, understanding your motivators, etc.) much more effectively. Thus, there are useful practical 21st century applications also to this 5000-years-old science.

## TO THINK AND DO THIS WEEK

### THINK

What is your favourite predictor of the future? How do you crystal-gaze?

### DO

Write some letters this week, from your future self ten years down the line, to your nearest and dearest ones, including yourself. Observe how your viewpoints change in time.

Experience:

Learnings:

Challenges:

WEEK 32

# NEUROPLASTICITY

*'Among other things, neuroplasticity means that emotions such as happiness and compassion can be cultivated in much the same way that a person can learn through repetition to play golf and basketball or master a musical instrument, and that such practice changes the activity and physical aspects of specific brain areas.'*

ANDREW WEIL

## THE CONTEXT

This week's fascinating enquiry – NEUROPLASTICITY – has been a source of continuous enquiry for us, given that Eika and I take pride in nurturing our grey cells. Neuroplasticity is essentially the ability of the brain to rewire and learn and grow. There is a substantial body of knowledge on this subject in both ancient wisdom and cutting-edge medical research.

## THE PROCESS

The timing of this RedPill, as well as the learnings of this week across both ancient wisdom and latest research, was massively inspired by attending a learning master class by Joey Hubbard (global head of training for Thrive Global). Thank you, Dr Marcus Ramney (India head for Thrive Global) for inviting us to an evening of fabulous conversation.

## THE LEARNINGS

1) According to our Vedas, the four faculties of the mind – *manas* (experience), *viveka* (analysis/judgement), *chitta* (memory) and *aham* (ego) – are rewired and altered (in varying degrees) with every experience. That is to say, a constant processing and reprocessing of the mind takes place, some consciously but mostly in an unconscious manner. The process of deliberate conscious rewiring for greater efficiency is accelerated by meditation. The silence of the *Turiya* or Alpha State or *Rithambara* allows for old impressions to fall off, and fetters to be cast away, and for the will of the consciousness to play through and strengthen newer neural pathways, subtly and surely.

2) We have heard the phrase, *Asatoma Sat Gamaya, Tamasoma Jyotir Gamaya* – the taking away of darkness happens only with replacement with light, and falsehoods don't go away, they just get replaced with truth. The universe doesn't believe in vacuums, so one's attention needs to be brought in for positive affirmation. The behaviour, attitude and value that you want to create must be worked upon with diligence. And like any other principle of strength training, neural pathways, thoughts, behaviours and attitudes that are not exercised and worked out, slowly atrophy. To give an analogy: the coal that doesn't get stoked becomes ash, and the one that is fuelled burns strong and bright.

3) Neuroplasticity in practice enables the formation of new neural pathways and the latest medical research says that new cells get fired up till late into middle age. So the old catechism does not necessarily hold true. You can absolutely teach an old dog new tricks!

The key to leverage neuroplasticity is to practice behaviour change. A simple rule of thumb that we consistently heard is that it takes between 16 and 66 days to embed a new habit or a sustained behaviourial change. We used this learning in our week to change our sleep timings to retire at 10 p.m. rather than by midnight (to enable an earlier start to the day). And we can safely say we are well on the path to rearranging our neural pathways.

We will be reading up more on Paul Brown's three-step process of neuroplasticity for further insights on behaviour change activation:

1) Becoming Aware,
2) Focussed Attention and
3) Repetitive Behaviour

## RESOURCES

- The books on neuroplasticity by Dr Paul Brown
- A useful article: https://positivepsychology.com/neuroplasticity/
- A set of fabulous videos on neuroplasticity on www.TED.com
- Online resources at www.ThriveGlobal.com remain a favourite for us.

## TO THINK AND DO THIS WEEK

### THINK

What are some behaviours, your own and in others, that irk and irritate you? Why?

________________________________________

________________________________________

________________________________________

### DO

Pick any one habit that you would like to change or cultivate in yourself. Create its new neural pathway this week by practicing it daily and through positive affirmation. Ideally, see if you can continue to practice and repeat the behaviours for another two weeks.

________________________________________

________________________________________

Experience:

________________________________________

________________________________________

Learnings:

________________________________________

________________________________________

Challenges:

________________________________________

________________________________________

WEEK 33

# THE THEORY OF EVERYTHING

*'Everything is interconnected.*
*My interest is linked to everyone else's.*
*Our survival and future are linked.'*

DALAI LAMA

## THE CONTEXT

This week's conversations revolved around THE THEORY OF EVERYTHING. In essence, we discussed the interconnectedness of everything. This is linked with the core philosophy of 52RedPills and, hence, is an important reason why some or most of our nuggets resonate with us, and are relevant to people's lives.

## THE PROCESS AND THE LEARNINGS

1) We used the system of *vaad vivaad* (debate) to unearth and discuss multiple perspectives. The discussions around the topic of interconnectedness grew richer and then escalated, with provocative topics such as the Jews descending from Lord Krishna's Yadav gene pool to Sun Tzu's *Art Of War*

being an inspired classic from Chankaya's *Arthashastra* – all part of an intense knowledge *baithak* (gathering) curated by Eika. And why not? We had an eclectic melting pot of intellectual powerhouses over lunch – a retired IIM-Bangalore professor, a bestselling author on mythology, a semiotics and design-thinking expert, a retired chemical engineer, the CEO of a production house, one of India's most successful content guru couple, an aura healer and several ardent students of ancient wisdom (some of them part of Eika's team of ancient wisdom researchers). A substantial cache of research material for our subsequent RedPills also emerged from this week's efforts. In corporate speak, we managed to do massive brainstorming with a diverse set of participants over briefs and hypotheses that were quite flexible in nature.

2) Ancient India understood interconnectedness well, and believed that the structure of the universe exists in each one of us. A key example to understand this was the interdisciplinary nature of studies at the *gurukuls* (schools), which was very different from the silo-styled education curricula of today. Kids entered a *gurukul* before the onset of puberty, anywhere between five to eight years of age. They studied philosophy, life and texts as a whole, and not as isolated sciences and disciplines. They also learnt the arts and logistics of leading the *grihasta* (householder) life.

   Hence, in the *Mahabharata*, that is how during the *agyatavasa* (unknown) period, Bhima was able to masquerade as a sous chef (Vallabha) and Arjun as a dance teacher (Brihanalla), essentially, taking advantage of the skills they had acquired during their early years.

It was only in the middle teens that the students could dive into their super specialization area of interest. Thus, Bhima was a war strategist, and a mace (*gada*) expert, and Arjun specialized in archery. Their superpower specialist discipline knowledge emerged from within the context of their understanding of life and living.

3) Consider another example from ancient India: Homeopathy, a process where the diagnosis is made through the interconnectedness of our emotional, intellectual, spiritual and physical bodies. That's how your homeopathic doctor spends the first two hours with you: understanding your dreams, fears, food tastes and cravings, desires, ambitions and everything else you cannot even imagine being related to your skin allergy. The doctor may also figure out that the root cause of your gynaecological issues and your sinusitis issues is the same, and, thus, prescribe the same medicine for both! Your mother, however, may get an absolutely different course of treatment for *her* sinusitis. That's interconnected medicine for you!

We follow this learning of interconnectedness in terms of 'a healthy body in a healthy mind' paradigm, which means that if we try to always have a positive mind frame, it will reflect on how we feel physically. The alternative has also played out for us in the past few weeks, where, sometimes, our stress has led us to feeling physically drained and tired.

A few lines on our interconnectedness from the poetess, Nikita Gill: 'We have calcium in our bones, iron in our veins, carbon in our souls, and nitrogen in our brains. Ninety-three per cent stardust, with souls made of flames, we are all just stars that have people names.'

As American astronomer Carl Sagan said: 'The cosmos is within us. We are made of star-stuff. We are a way for the universe to know itself.'

## RESOURCES

- The writings of The Dalai Lama
- *A Short History of Nearly Everything* by Bill Bryson.
- Stephen Hawking on our quest for a theory of everything: www.brainpickings.org/2018/08/20/stephen-hawking-a-brief-history-of-time-theory/

## TO THINK AND DO THIS WEEK

### THINK

What is your favourite theory of the universe, your core philosophy that explains everything?

### DO

Explore philosophy this week, Western, Eastern and the Oriental. Discover which aligns closest to your own thought process and belief systems.

Experience:

Learnings:

Challenges:

WEEK 34

# CHANNELLING ENERGY

*'This achieving the centre, being grounded in one's self, is about the highest state a human being can achieve.'*

BRUCE LEE

## THE CONTEXT

This week's enquiry is fascinating since it is about who we are; essentially, forms of energy. Hence, CHANNELING ENERGY is what we spent time researching and discussing.

## THE PROCESS

Our starting point came from Yuval Noah Harari's bestselling book, *Sapiens*, in which he speaks of the journey of human evolution actually being the journey of discovery of newer sources of energy – fire, solar, electricity, magnetism, potential, kinetic, hydro, wind and turbine, fossil fuels et al. Harari then proposes a provocation about the possibility of the human mind being the ultimate source and catalytic converter of energy. And that got us excited!

What can we do about this? And from where do we learn more about it? Well, ancient wisdom, it seems, had already cracked this code.

## THE LEARNINGS

1) **Consider Yoga:** There are over a 125 *chakra*s or energy centres identified in the human body, as per yoga. Of these, the seven main *chakras* are located along the spinal cord. Think of them as energy nodes, where the gross body (*sthula sharira*), the subtle body (*sukshma sharira*), and the energy body (*atma*) meet, in exchange and control of the motor, emotional and intellectual transactions of the body. These seven are:
   - The Root or *Mooladhara* Chakra, associated with basic trust and safety.
   - The Sacral or *Swadisthana* Chakra, associated with sexuality and creativity.
   - The Solar Plexus or *Manipura* Chakra, associated with wisdom and power.
   - The Heart or *Anahata* Chakra, associated with love and healing.
   - The Throat or *Vishuddha* Chakra, associated with communication and expression.
   - The Third Eye or *Ajna* Chakra, associated with awareness and intuition.
   - The Crown or *Sahastrara* Chakra, associated with spirituality and consciousness.

   Disease and illnesses are all related to the disturbances in the alignment of these *chakras*. And every 'alternative' discipline of health and wellness – Ashtanga yoga, Hatha yoga, pranayama, asana, *dhyana* (meditation), reiki, and pranic healing – are all based on the principles of *chakra* healing and alignment. This is one of India's gifts to the world that we all need to embrace more. Such is the holistic power of this practice. Eika is a living example of the benefits of Yoga – having healed herself of her chronic sinusitis and frozen hip, as well as PTSD and a broken heel and knee after a particularly nasty hit-and-run road accident – all through yoga, *dhyana* (meditation), and *pranayama* (breathing).

2) **Understand your *Kundalini*:** No, this is not an *en vogue* ancient word; this can be a life-changing discovery for a lucky few. *Kundalini* is the latent energy that lies coiled at the base of the spine, and as *chakras* come in absolute perfect alignment of their natural frequencies and cohesion, the *kundalini* slowly uncoils and rises, *chakra* by *chakra*, to finally unlock at the crown, the *sahastrara*, in resonance, and the *sadhak* (practitioner) then becomes one with the super consciousness, the *paramatma*, in blissful *samadhi* (union).

3) **Appreciate Tai Chi:** The Chinese wisdom speaks of 'chi', the universal energy. Thus Tai Chi is the 'way of the energy'. It is, basically, the discipline of aligning the body's energy flow in harmony with itself, and with the universal consciousness of the yin and yang. The yin and yang rotates while the core reverts to stillness.Tai Chi is also the base discipline for learning most martial arts such as kung fu and wushu. Eika recently practiced Tai Chi with her team at an offsite and could feel the difference in her energy flow almost immediately.

Both the concept of *chakras* and *chi* are about harnessing the energy of the universe for health and longevity at the minimum; advanced practitioners can control external mind and bodies too. If these disciplines interest you, find a well-known, certified expert and spend a week or two understanding the basics. If you find fulfilment in the first few days, you might want to integrate one of these practices into your daily life.

**Caveat:** We are just learning the basics of these practices and till Eika and I spend time at a monastery sometime in life, we continue to learn little by little from the master-trainers in our network.

## RESOURCES

- 'Be Water, My Friend', a YouTube video on Bruce Lee's famous life philosophy.
- *Zen and the Art of Motorcycle Maintenance: An Inquiry Into Values* by Robert M. Pirsig
- 'Anatomy of the Spirit: The Seven Stages of Power and Healing' by Caroline Myss

## TO THINK AND DO THIS WEEK

### THINK

What is your Zen practice? How do you best expend and channelize your energy?

### DO

Pick up a new physical or mental activity this week. You can choose cooking, baking, pottery, carpentry, painting, sketching, knitting, stitching, yoga, pranayama, Tai Chi or anything else that interests you.

Experience:

Learnings:

Challenges:

WEEK 35

# THE SCIENCE OF CONSCIOUSNESS

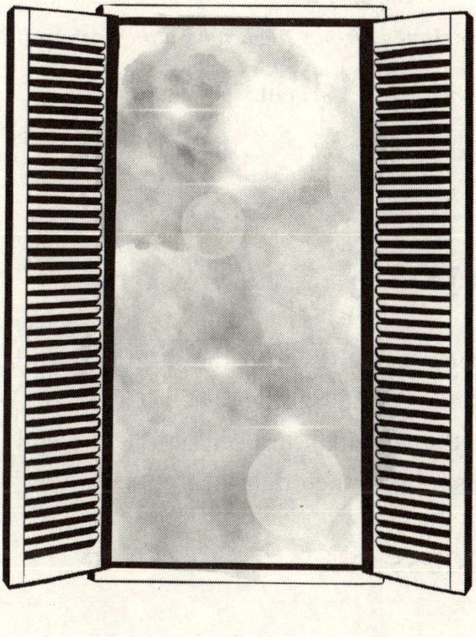

*'God does not play dice with the universe.'*

ALBERT EINSTEIN

*'Not only does God play dice but ...*
*he sometimes throws them where they cannot be seen.'*

STEPHEN HAWKING

## THE CONTEXT

We threw ourselves into the deep end with this week's RedPill – THE SCIENCE OF CONCIOUSNESS – an enquiry that spans quantum physics at one end and ancient Vedic philosophy at the other.

## THE PROCESS

We had multiple chats on this subject with practitioners who have explored this path, and we were lucky enough to get our wise friend Anuraag Agarwal as a guide and sounding board. (Amongst his many sterling qualities is the fact that he is also a fellow Martinian, from the same school as mine.)

## THE LEARNINGS

Why is this relevant to us? What is the practical application of this abstruse knowledge? Want to know about ways to understand one's true self and to deal with desires, vicissitudes, illness and negative thoughts?

1) The core philosophical underpinnings of the movie *Matrix* appear aligned with and inspired by our ancient wisdom. We are all space, the material called Brahman that is composed of *sat* (truth; it knows and exists), *chit* (conscious; it's alive) and *anand* (bliss). But we do not perceive the world in that way because our senses have limitations. Perception becomes our reality (*jaisi dhristhi, vaisi shrishti*). In a simplified form, all our perceptions are nothing but the awareness of the moving particles. These keep changing and are not reflective of our true nature, hence, not 'real'. And when you try to find it again, it's not there in the same way again. Thus, the delusion when we try to keep finding the same joy or sorrow from an object, person or situation. If we could still the moving particles or shift our awareness to the space instead of the moving particles, we could experience the space. And, thereby, experience our true nature. We can experience *sat*, *chit* and *anand*. The essence of spirituality is to train ourselves to perceive and observe this space, and, in doing so, become closer to own true selves.

   The toolbox for doing this is threefold: Asanas, Pranayam and Meditation.

   In the Art Of Living (AOL) construct, which we learnt post immersing ourselves in an AOL course, this can be further developed by *sadhana (*practice), *sewa* (service) and *satsang* (community devotion). Eika has managed to weave meditation into her daily life and she benefits from the clarity of mind that this practice affords her.

2) I Am Not a Body, Only Waves: The core of Vedanta is 'I create my own reality'. Since my true nature is *sat chit anand*, my true state is that of bliss, which is how we are as children. However, as all of us are 'socialized' and conditioned, we forget our essential selves and fall into the trap of the outer electron world, rather than the Brahman. The mantra is: 'The mind creates its own drama. The strongest thought wins.' If you think you are coming down with fever, you probably will fall ill. If you are dreading something, your worst fears will possibly be realized. The submission is, have clarity of your intentions, enjoy the journey and the destination will work itself out (in due course of time).

3) Of Desires and the Impermanence of Happiness: Remember the last time you got something you really wanted? The joy of getting to that desire would have lasted a day or two, and then the mind would have got focussed on the next desire. So, the joy is temporary. And desire, as the condition for human happiness, is the root cause of all problems. Hence, the submission is to have dreams and desires, but don't get attached to them. And if you are having negative thoughts, relax and understand that joy is an inner state of being rather than object dependent.

**The mantra is:** Be happy and act, rather than act for happiness.

## TO THINK AND DO THIS WEEK

THINK

What would you like to forget and whom would you like to forgive?

DO

Practice letting go of at least one desire. As discussed in the neuroplasticity RedPill earlier, in order to let go, you will need to create an alternate neural pathway. So, what are you replacing your desire with is important.

Experience:

Learnings:

Challenges:

WEEK 36

# BUILDING MENTAL RESILIENCE

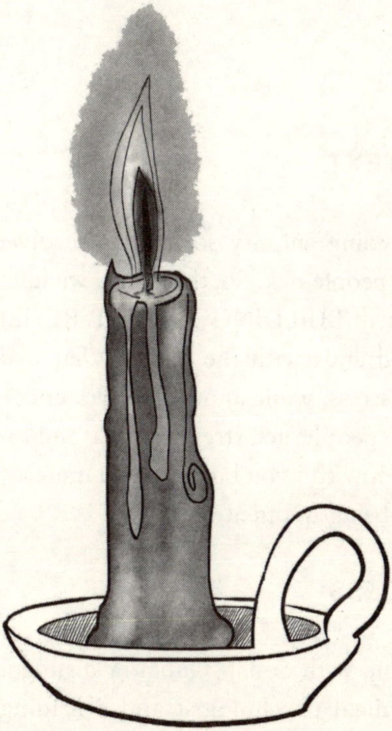

*'Fall 99 times, rise 100.'*

JAPANESE PROVERB

## THE CONTEXT

Our on-going enquiry so far has revolved around what makes people tick. So, this week, we immersed ourselves into the area of BUILDING MENTAL RESILIENCE, since it all starts and ends with the mind. What makes one person crack under stress, while another thrives under pressure? Why do so many people get stress-related and/or heart diseases these days? How can you build mental muscle to increase your overall well-being quotient?

## THE PROCESS

We spent time with Sonali Gupta, a distinguished and well-regarded clinical psychologist and a leading consultant to several organizations on matters related to well being. Our conversation traversed the understanding of the human brain, psychological concepts and modern-day relationships that have been impacted by technology.

## THE LEARNINGS

- Most of us live in a 'super-wired' world, where we constantly operate from our reptilian brain, and our limbic system seems to stay perpetually in a state of fight, flight or freeze. The primitive caveman used to get stressed at the sight of a mammoth or sabre-toothed tiger. The same stress for the modern-day human is generated by an office email or a nasty WhatsApp message. So be careful of technology and recognize who is the master and who is the slave.
- Sonali calls this state of stress and anxiety a 'state of slow burn', where people crumble from the inside since they don't nourish their inner selves. A simple tip is to breathe, relax and allow yourself to be in a state of rest. Self-care and self-replenishment is the antidote to slow burn.
- A key reason for stress is psycho-social set-ups, where people are cut off from real social relationships. This happens when social media takes over and when people prefer to text rather than call. This is on the rise with people across age groups and gender.
- How does one recognize that emotional resilience needs to be worked upon? According to Sonali, 'As a psychologist I feel, all of us have emotional resilience. We can work towards strengthening it.'

Here are factors that make people vulnerable and in turn impact their resilience:

- Difficulty regulating emotions (anger issues, road rage and anxiety flashes)
- Breakdown of close relationships
- Substance addiction, and
- Suicidal thoughts

That is when you should immediately reach out for help and work towards strengthening resilience.

- Mental resilience is about being in touch with yourself. It is our capacity to 'bounce back' from difficult situations and trust that we can cope even with overwhelming situations. One of the ways to do this is by processing emotions, which involves awareness of and feeling the emotion and then unpacking it.
- In summary, Sonali's three tips to increase mental resilience are:
  1) Develop self-compassion and factor in time for your own physical and emotional self-care.
  2) Learn to recognize yourself (your limits, boundaries and triggers). For example, a colleague recognized that responding to her emails and messages within a minute of receiving them was a (hidden) trigger for stress.
  3) Research has shown that exercise, mindfulness-based meditation and increased social support all add to our resilience.
  4) The important narrative for organizations and schools is to build structural resilience that allows individuals to work better and take care of their own health.

## RESOURCES

- Sonali's YouTube channel for more learnings in this discipline.
  https://youtu.be/Vgf270W_RWo

## TO THINK AND DO THIS WEEK

This is an exercise which Sonali often uses with clients in therapy.

### THINK

What triggers stress for you? Ask yourself how it impacts you.

---

---

---

### DO

Identify whether it's work overload, technology, relationships or your own habits (overthinking) that trigger stress in you?

Then write down its impact on your body, thoughts and behaviour.

---

---

Experience:

---

---

Learnings:

---

---

Challenges:

---

---

WEEK 37

# ON IKIGAI

*'Only staying active will make you want to live a hundred years.'*

JAPANESE PROVERB

## THE CONTEXT

This week's RedPill on IKIGAI is a part of Eika and my constant discussions in 2018. And we were fortunate to explore and discuss the Ikigai concept in detail with Singapore-based Nandini Das Ghoshal, an insights entrepreneur, respected coach, and our friend for the past three decades.

## THE PROCESS

Nandini coaches organizations and individuals using Ikigai principles, and it was a delight to understand this topic with her audio notes, one-pagers and PowerPoint slides. She also transcribed our entire learning discussion wonderfully, as given below. Thank you, Nandini!

## THE LEARNINGS

Ikigai became a hot topic after Dan Beuttner, a *National Geographic* writer and explorer brought it to the fore with his TED talk. In his video, he talked about the secret to the longevity of people who live in 'blue zones', where community elders could live to 100 years. This interesting TED talk went viral with 3.4 million views and was transcribed in 32 languages since it was first aired in 2010.

Dan, however, was not the originator of this concept. Ikigai, as an idea, has existed in Japan for thousands of years.

Translated, Ikigai essentially means 'the reason for being', the thing that makes life worthwhile. In its most popular modern-day representation, it consists of four concentric circles. 'What we love' and 'what we are good at' magically overlap with 'what the world values' and 'what we can be paid for'. Hence, it implies that we can do something that the world values and is willing to pay for, and this makes our lives purposeful.

The original Japanese concept was different. As per that, one's Ikigai may have nothing to do with income. In fact, in a survey of 2000 Japanese men and women conducted by Central Research Services in 2010, just 31 per cent of recipients considered work as their Ikigai. Someone's value in life can be work, but is indeed not limited to that. In 1966, psychiatrist Mieko Kamiya tried to contextualize this ancient term to modern times. His idea was that Ikigai was similar to happiness, but with a subtle difference in its nuance. Ikigai is what allows you to look forward to the future even if you're miserable right now. Ikigai has the essential elements of action (doing what you love) and state of mind (feeling good doing it) combined within it.

Since 2010, this framework has caught the imagination of millions across the world. It could be because this period has coincided with the rise of entrepreneurship, 'solo-preneurship' and the gig economy as a valid way of livelihood. Many in this world are spurred by individual vision, the need to find their purpose, to live a life where passion becomes profession and finally, a need to express themselves; or in other words, to be the heroes of their own stories. Ikigai's compelling promise, thus, is that of unlocking positive energy, wonder, hope and bliss.

In visual terms, imagine Ikigai as your own space (a dojo, studio or a workshop), where you have your own tools that add purpose and meaning to your life, and with which you can wow the world.

How to think of Ikigai? If one looks at its concentric circles closely, one can see that 'what we love' and 'what are we good at' fall in the zone of man's internal world. He is answerable to no one for these two zones. The other two circles are 'what the world values' and 'what we can be paid for'. These two belong to the external world. Most adults adjusted in the daily rhythm of life would actually be 'at Ikigai' or hovering close by.

The problem arises when the context of the existing world changes, when the world that is VUCA (Volatile, Uncertain, Complex and Ambiguous) rears its ugly head and, suddenly, what the world values is not the same. Hence, we cannot be paid for what we were doing earlier. The Ikigai is no longer relevant. The equilibrium has shifted. This results in deep disturbance, confusion, lack of control, anxiety and even despair and breakdown. To emerge from this, one has to redefine one's Ikigai according to the new normal.

One has to relook at one's internal world, and, essentially, reach within to the two circles of what one loves and what one is good at, and its intersection. One can work on what one loves to bring it to what one is good at. Many musicians, dancers and artists can relate to this story. However, it need not be restricted to the arts. People who understand money and investments can work on it to make it a profession. Those good at cooking can train to be a chef. Those good at teaching can make it into a profession. The possibilities are immense. It is about examining our inner world and seeing what we can pull out. And then working on it to turn it into a 'skill'. This journey of strengthening a talent is the journey of redefining one's Ikigai.

Natural talents blur over the years due to socialization or being part of a team that was put together to achieve a corporate purpose. However, once out of that context, an individual need not feel hopeless or unsupported. Our inner world is rich with hidden talents and possibilities. What is most important is to keep building one's strengths and adding to the Ikigai. There will be a period of pulling out old plugs, looking at existing talents and polishing them up. But an individual will always be able to find new Ikigai if he or she just keeps at it.

An essential pit stop here may be dealing with three barriers: lack of self-awareness, self-doubt (fear and anxiety) and self-conditioning (attachment to old frames of reference). Self-awareness and acknowledgement of these existing mental patterns can equip us to take the next steps. What one does need is plenty of grit and a willingness to work on the time-consuming process of discovering one's Ikigai. As Angela Duckworth says in her book, *Grit Trumps Talent*. Talent applied with effort is skill. This combination will ensure that we are able to redefine our Ikigai.

The net conclusion is that Ikigai is NOT a fixed place. It is a dynamic, iterative process that keeps bringing us to our centre. And it is from this place that we will always find the essential material for new growth and fresh avenues. The above explanation is a practical approach to regaining one's own space when one is displaced due to changes in the external environment.

## FIVE TIPS TO RE-SPARK YOUR IKIGAI

1. Recognize your talents and passions, not only from recent times, but also from the past. Take an inventory and earmark the ones that can be developed into skills or strengths.
2. Scope out opportunity in the larger world and identify addressable people, organizations, and groups, where you can manifest your new skill.
3. Start your journey by abandoning the need to be perfect from day one. This relates to the Japanese notion of Wabi Sabi, which is about embracing imperfection, the unfinished and the transient.
4. Start to build your skill by putting effort into your talents not used hitherto. Keep pushing ahead till you attain mastery. (Note: The combination of two or more skills can create a unique niche for you.)
5. Allow yourself to ease into a new identity with your new ability, one practice at a time.

We hope this helps in your journey to find or reinvent your own Ikigai.

## TO THINK AND DO THIS WEEK

### THINK

What is your own current Ikigai chart? Make one for yourself?

### DO

Visit and revisit your favourite TED Talks this week, one a day. Share them on your social media feeds along with your comments, thoughts and views.

Experience:

Learnings:

Challenges:

WEEK 38

# THE PROCESS OF SCIENTIFIC DISCOVERY

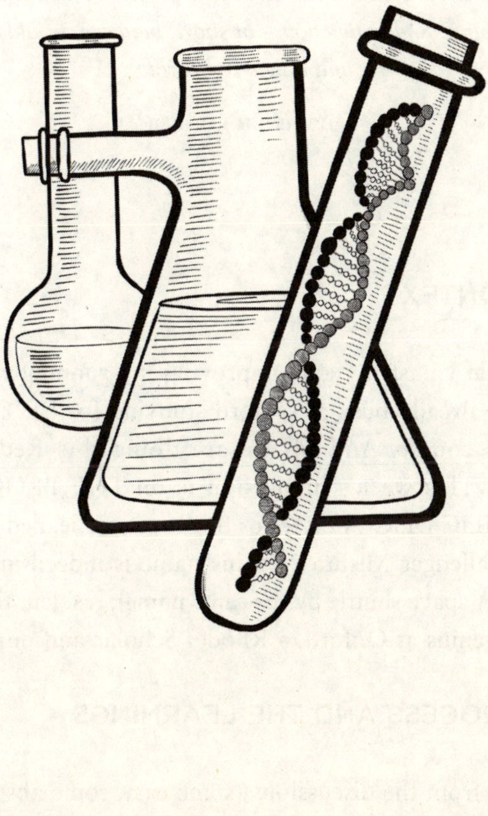

*'Science means constantly walking a tightrope between blind faith and curiosity; between expertise and creativity; between bias and openness; between experience and epiphany; between ambition and passion; and between arrogance and conviction – in short, between an old today and a new tomorrow.'*

HEINRICH ROHRER

## THE CONTEXT

While I bust my guts improving my running time, Eika is already busy at Oxford studying for her Chevening Gurukul course. And so, we are doing this RedPill long distance. This week's immersion is on THE PROCESS OF SCIENTIFIC DISCOVERY. For this topic, we leaned on inputs from Challenger Mishra (yes, his name is indeed inspired by the NASA space shuttle by the same name), resident theoretical physics genius at Oxford, a Rhodes Scholar and our friend.

## THE PROCESS AND THE LEARNINGS

Excerpts from the discussions (some easy, some abstruse):

The process of certain scientific discoveries can be thought of as being based on the three basic principles of Empiricism, Scepticism, and Creativity.

- Empiricism can be thought of as comprising of Observation (of phenomenon), tracking for Patterns, and the subsequent formulation of an Idea or a Conjecture that could possibly explain the observation and the pattern.
- Scepticism then examines the inference or the conjecture that emerges from the empirical evidence, through the lens of falsifiability, predictability and reproducibility. These are necessary criteria for the conjecture to lift to the status of a universally accepted theory. Since empiricism focuses on evidence-based inference generation, it fails when it comes to generating new ideas that are about reality, but outside the scope of our sensory experiences. There is a plethora of such examples in modern theoretical physics. How then does one discover such theoretical descriptions of reality? A theoretical physicist attempting to formulate a theory that describes reality without the luxury of experimental data replaces empiricism by Creativity.
- Creativity, although limitless in its potential, is chaperoned by strong mathematical frameworks and guiding principles tying together all physical phenomena. One such guiding principle is the notion of preservation of symmetry that draws equivalence between fundamental physical phenomena and the safeguarding of certain symmetries of the universe.

The fundamental principles governing our universe manifests differently in different frames of references. It is only through our understanding of how these different manifestations transform into one another that we come to realize that fundamental governing principle. In modern theoretical physics, this is equivalent to discovering the symmetries of our universe.

Meanwhile, the ancient Indian wisdom construct actually details out the process of creativity, as we understand in science, through the process of conscious mindfulness or *dhyana*. Swami Vivekanand, too, talks about the process of 'discovery' as opposed to 'invention'. We already 'know' the process of life and science. We only need to 'unveil' them. Like Piyush Pandey had said in one of our earlier 52RedPills, insights come from observing honestly and without judgements. The same seems to be applicable for something as left brained as theoretical physics. Hence, Scepticism, too, needs to be as validating as it is falsifying. So, you can't be just a naysayer. Even String Theory has not found the perfect vacuum.

Going back to our earlier 52RedPill on positive affirmation, it is not possible to just NOT do something. There has to be a positive replacement.

## RESOURCES

- *Fearful Symmetry* by Anthony Zee
- *The Beginning of Infinity* by David Deutsche

## TO THINK AND DO THIS WEEK

### THINK

What does technology or scientific advancement mean to you?

________________________________________

________________________________________

________________________________________

### DO

Pick your favourite latest technology application – medical, engineering, automobile, construction, home installation, infrastructure or anything else. Decode the process of its evolution and predict a possible future.

________________________________________

________________________________________

________________________________________

Experience:

________________________________________

________________________________________

Learnings:

________________________________________

________________________________________

Challenges:

________________________________________

________________________________________

WEEK 39

# BHAGWAD GITA, THE SOURCE CODE OF MANAGEMENT

*'Access to the Vedas is the greatest privilege this century may claim over all previous centuries.'*

J. ROBERT OPPENHEIMER

## THE CONTEXT

This week marks the 75 per cent *done* milestone of our 52 weeks' journey. And we celebrated with an exploration into the fascinating world of the *BHAGWAD GITA*, THE SOURCE CODE OF MANAGEMENT, possibly. We would encourage everybody to read and assimilate this text, as it is replete with thought-provoking questions.

## THE PROCESS

Eika and I are fortunate that several Vedic scholars have shared their views on the *Mahabharata*, *Bhagwad Gita*, Vedanta philosophy and so on with us over this year. Eika also enjoyed a conversation over tea with Shaunaka Rishi Das (born Tadgh MacTighearnan), the director of the Oxford Centre for Hindu Studies (OCHS), to glean a different, informed perspective also.

## THE LEARNINGS

- The magic of the *Bhagwad Gita* is that it is as if almost all of the world's philosophy has been contextualized to a narrative and a story that makes it easy to disseminate. So, it serves almost like a handy guide and lighthouse, if you apply it well.
- The *Bhagwad Gita*, literally translated as the 'Song of God', is a broad-minded pluralist text, presented as an opinion by Lord Krishna to Arjun, the man standing in front of him, espousing a non-dogmatic concept of 'choice' to love, rather than love as an obligation. Arjun has the eternal choice of loving Krishna. And Krishna does not separate the head from the heart, or philosophy from theology. Krishna, thus, is the new idea of the common God, a generous, open God.
- The *Gita* flows at the level of the Thought, Action and Emotion.

1) ***Samadarshana*****:** the Principle - the Attitude - the Gyan - the Thought - the What

   This is the principle of equal vision. It states that every life form is equal spiritually, even if not materially, which allows for equitable treatment for each other. The present legal system is based on the specist construct of human dignity. *Samadarshana* is non-specist. This applies to our environment, economics and political structures, too. The question it raised for us: Is there merit in *samadarshana* becoming the basis of our legal system?

2) **Ahimsa:** the Value – the Karma – the Action – the How: non-violation in our actions and words.

   Abusing, debasing and aggression towards any other human are all acts of violence, and, deriving from *samadarshana*, also towards our environment and all life forms. Bullying is violence. As is spreading misinformation, calling a woman fat or a politician lying, and so on. *Ahimsa* or not causing distress is the basis for *dharma*, your code of action.

3) **Priti:** the Virtue – the Bhakti – the Emotion – the Why:

   *Priti* is kindness in thought and action. Everyone is looking to give and receive love, so maybe there is some eternal truth to the acclaimed Beatles' song. 'Love Is All You Need'. And it is in our ability to give love. *Priti* both drives and is derived from *samadarshana* and *ahimsa*. And *Priti* is the sole underlying human value and virtue; all else derives from here.

Approaching all of one's thoughts and actions in the consciousness of the why, what and how of emotion, action and attitude or, indeed, just living in awareness of the Self is *ananda*, a state of perpetual bliss, above and beyond the daily happiness and sadness.

## TO THINK AND DO THIS WEEK

### THINK

Which are your favourite non-fiction books?

____________________________________________________________________________

____________________________________________________________________________

____________________________________________________________________________

____________________________________________________________________________

### DO

Study and examine six teachings across any 'religious' text – the Bhagwad Gita, Bible, Quran or any other. Examine them for their philosophies, similarities and differences.

____________________________________________________________________________

____________________________________________________________________________

____________________________________________________________________________

Experience:

____________________________________________________________________________

____________________________________________________________________________

Learnings:

____________________________________________________________________________

____________________________________________________________________________

Challenges:

____________________________________________________________________________

____________________________________________________________________________

WEEK 40

# COMMUNICATING EFFECTIVELY

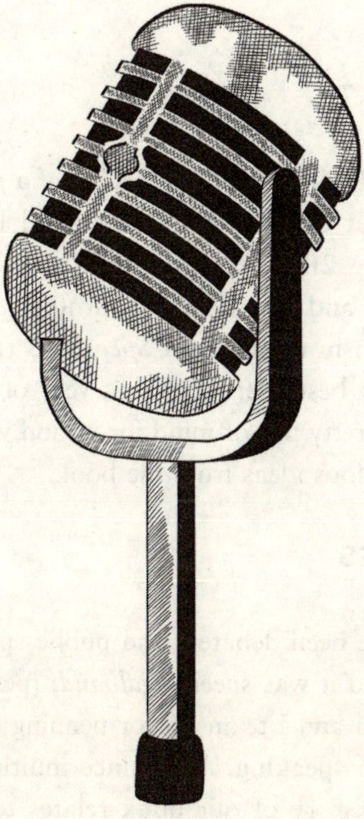

*'Friends, Romans, countrymen, lend me your ears.'*

MARK ANTONY IN *JULIUS CAESAR*, WILLIAM SHAKESPEARE

## THE CONTEXT

This week's RedPill is a culmination of a *junoon* (passion) of a project that Roshan Abbas and I had embarked on in February 2017, the idea of COMMUNICATING EFFECTIVELY, and the dream of turning it into a book. It came to fruition in the form of *Speechless* (released in 2018 and an Amazon bestseller in its first year of launch). Hence, this RedPill is pretty top-of-mind for us and we celebrated the week with fabulous ideas from the book.

## THE PROCESS

Eika and I have been debaters and public speakers in school and college. And it was sheer *jugalbandi* (perfect duet) when she saw Roshan and I team up for penning India's definitive book on public speaking. Also, since multiple friends have asked, the backstory of our book relates to the Speechless Workshop that Roshan and I conducted in Stream 2017 at

Jaipur to a standing ovation (the attached picture is a nod to that moment), a lot of love and good feedback. Thank you to our friend Apoorva Bapna, the prime mover behind this fabulous annual event.

So why is it so important to communicate effectively?

- The ancient Greeks and Romans supported 'Four Rs' as compulsory skills: Reading, Writing, Arithmetic and Rhetoric. While most of us would have heard about the first three, rhetoric has literally fallen off the map. Communicating effectively, however, is a very important life skill and an advantage for anybody, since we are all selling ideas at most times, in the form of a business presentation, a VC pitch, a love proposal, a call to arms in a war or in a corporate team context.
- Roshan and I have based our book on a simple mantra known as SPEECHLESS, where each of the ten letters stand for a particular action point in order to ensure two things:
  - Never be left speechless (LOGIC steps) and
  - Speak in a manner that leaves your audience speechless with awe (MAGIC steps).

The rationale behind Logic and Magic was simple. We felt everybody should learn the basics of effective communication so that they are never speechless in front of an audience. And so, these steps are prescriptive, and the outcomes are effective and efficient.

Truthfully speaking, some of the steps are basic common sense: Preparation, Highlighting, Summary and so on. But we have brought it alive through our public speaking experience over the last cumulative 50 years. Plus, interviews with experts such as Gaurav Kapur, Mini Mathur, Harsha Bhogle, Mandira

Bedi et al. ensure that the key messages land effectively and memorably.

## THE LEARNINGS

1) Prepare, Prepare, Prepare: The best speakers always do. They spend time and effort to know their audience, they research what will and will not resonate and they are ready with fallbacks. Steve Jobs was known to prepare intensely before his public presentations.
2) Be Yourself: Develop your own personal style. Whether you rehearse in front of a mirror or with a trusted friend, be aware of your delivery style and your energy levels. Do not copy anybody. Play to your strengths. The comedian Kapil Sharma is a great example of being himself and being great on stage.
3) Write, Reduce, Repeat. This is one of Roshan's favourite sayings. In essence, his callout is for you to make your ideas as succinct and simple as possible. Use the simple and oft-quoted phrase 'less is more'. Also, ensure that you repeat your thread or core premise a couple of times so that the audience is clear about your main message. TED calls this the 'throughline'. We are big fans of keeping it simple. One of *my* favourite tips is 'The Rule of 3', which is to distil your speech or presentation down to three key points.

In our book, I have specifically mentioned a saying by my schoolteacher: 'Your handwriting should be so clear that even a blind man can read it.' I argue the same holds true for effective communication. Your main message should be so crystal clear and powerful that it can never be missed.

Indra Nooyi, former CEO of PepsiCo, talks about her 5Cs for Corporate Success and mentions the C of (Clear) Communication as being critical. The video of her talk is available online and is a sheer delight to watch and learn.

**Note:** *We hope some of these nuggets inspire you to look up Speechless on Amazon (open for orders).*

## RESOURCES

- *Speechless* by Roshan Abbas and Siddharth Banerjee.
- *Ziglar on Selling* by Zig Ziglar.
- Check out Chris Andersen's book, *TED Talks* and his fabulous TED video below: www.ted.com/talks/chris_anderson_teds_secret_to_great_public_speaking/up-next?language=en

## TO THINK AND DO THIS WEEK

### THINK

Are you guilty of saying too many things or overloading in a presentation or a speech?

### DO

Practice the 'Rule of 3' in all your communication this week.

Experience:

Learnings:

Challenges:

WEEK 41

# HOW TO BEAT A HEART ATTACK

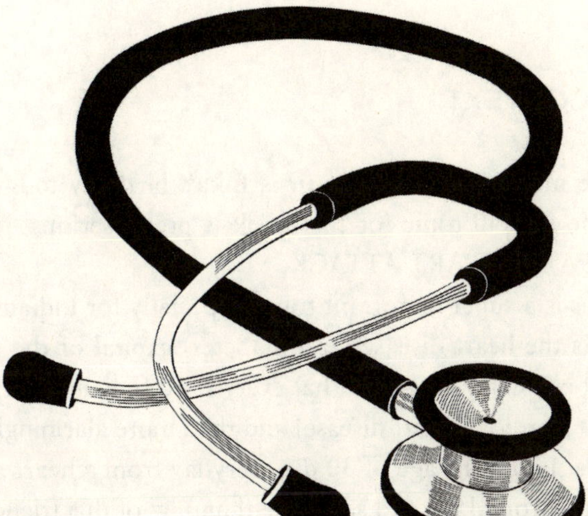

*'A light heart lives long.'*

WILLIAM SHAKESPEARE

## THE CONTEXT

The mood is celebratory (it is Eika's birthday today), but the RedPill topic for this week is pretty serious – HOW TO BEAT A HEART ATTACK.

This is a super-important topic, especially for Indians since India is the heart disease (and diabetes) capital of the world. Recent estimates suggested that every third Indian suffers from a CVD (cardiovascular disease) and that, more alarmingly, 900 Indians (under the age of 30 die everyday from a heart attack. We look around us, and see more than few of our friends and colleagues having heart attacks, most, unfortunately, fatal. And the level of information and misinformation around the subject is scary.

## THE PROCESS

To understand this topic better, we spoke to several cardiologists across Delhi, Mumbai and Bangalore over this week. An interesting revelation for us was that heart attacks are a modern-day disease. Our Ayurveda texts, which talk about diabetes (*madhu meha*) and tuberculosis (*chaya riga*) do not make mention of heart attacks as a killer disease. So what happened over the years and why do we see so many (young and apparently fit) people around us succumbing to heart attacks?

## THE LEARNINGS

- Modern-day urbanization, with all its attendant problems (physical inactivity, pollution, poisoned food chain etc.) has contributed to a looming health crisis, as far as CVDs and, specifically, heart attacks are concerned. Added to this are the current banes of smoking (which literally doubles the chances of a heart attack) and processed sugar (that can cause diabetes, a key risk factor for heart attacks). So, if you really want to beat a heart attack, becoming a farmer in the hills might not be a bad idea.
- Heart attacks cannot be predicted. They can, however, be prevented by understanding the risk factors. While some of them are non-modifiable (age, gender, race), others are modifiable. A basic list of the latter includes diabetes, smoking, hypertension, high cholesterol, family history, obesity, sedentary lifestyles, poor life habits (junk food, lack of sleep etc.) and stress. The first five risk factors are critical, and if applicable to you, be sure to make lifestyle changes accordingly.
- How does one beat a heart attack?

  Well, as it turns out, you can't. But think of it this way. Instead of standing in the middle of the road, you can move to the side and reduce the chances of an accident.

There are five simple ways to lower your risk factors, as proposed by the doctors we met:

1) Your annual medical check up is not enough to give assurance for a clean chit. Use it only for its preventive signals since the whole process is *not* predictive. As an ECG is 60 per cent and a TMT Stress/Echo Test is around 85–90 per cent indicative (by doctor estimates), practicing a regulated lifestyle is more useful than tests.
2) Do not smoke, and do not passively smoke. The latter is equally dangerous. Think of that at the next party you attend, while standing in a balcony with friends who are smoking around you.
3) Moderate exercise on a daily basis is non-negotiable. A 45-minutes daily walk is good. Not everybody needs to become a marathoner. (In case you do, remember to do so gradually.)
4) Diet and nutrition are key. Five small bowls of fresh fruits and vegetables daily (some call it the Mediterranean Diet) are good for the heart. Consume garlic, turmeric, almonds and walnuts in your meals. Drop sugar and refined carbohydrates (highly polished rice, *maida* etc.) from your diet. Instead, consider and explore our age-old balanced diet principles (30 per cent protein, 30 per cent fat and 30 per cent carbohydrates).

   P.S. There is a reason why grandma puts *desi ghee* on your *fulkaas*.
5) Every six months, keep a close tab on your core medical statistics – blood pressure, blood sugar, cholesterol levels etc.). Also, do download the ASCVD Risk Calculator app on your phone, which calculates one's estimated heart attack risk for the next ten years and make an action plan

for yourself. This is a core learning, from this week, that we have incorporated into our lives.

## RESOURCES

A BBC e-article on calculating your heart age:

www.bbc.com/news/health-45395576?ns_mchannel=social&ocid=socialflow_facebook&ns_campaign=bbcnews&ns_source=facebook

CAVEAT: We are not authorized medical professionals. So please treat this note as a mere catalyst to do your own research and learn.

## TO THINK AND DO THIS WEEK

### THINK

What are your risk factors? What are your mitigants?

### DO

This week, plan and go for your health check-up, along with the family. And replace refined oil in your cooking with any cold-pressed or virgin oil.

Experience:

Learnings:

Challenges:

WEEK 42

# THE SCIENCE BEHIND INDIAN FESTIVALS

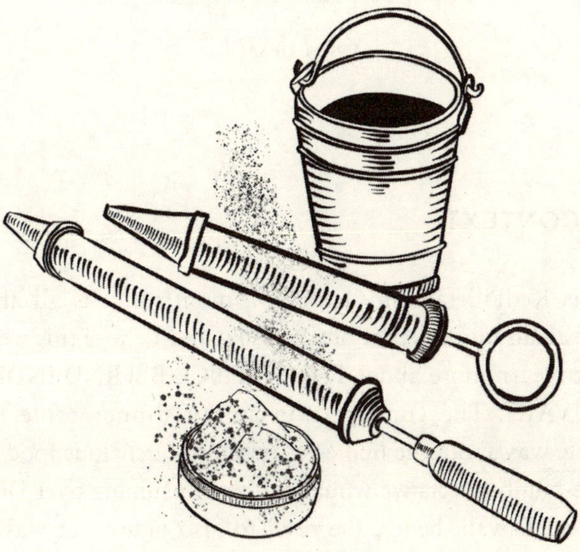

*'India is a curious place that still preserves its past, religions, and its history.*
*No matter how modern India becomes, it is still very much an old country.'*

ANITA DESAI

## THE CONTEXT

This RedPill falls in October, a month that is all about festivals and celebrations. So Eika and I chose this week's topic to learn more about THE SCIENCE BEHIND INDIAN FESTIVALS. The conversation at our dinner table, one evening, was about the immense amount of delicious food and calorie-bomb-sweets we would end up consuming over Durga Puja and Diwali; hence, the need to also figure out ways of moderation, including intermittent fasting. As we got into the food and fasting debates, we were super interested by the fact that ancient Indian rituals, based on biology and food science, supported intermittent fasting much before Western celebrities popularized the trend in the recent decade.

## THE PROCESS

We conducted some basic research across our readings; more interestingly, however, Eika and I engineered dinner-table conversations with our daughters on the subject. For the purposes of a simple discussion set-up, more than for any daily application (unlike our other 52RedPills), we broke it down to three aspects: agricultural cycles, health and wellness, and socio-cultural contexts.

## THE LEARNINGS

1) The Agricultural Cycles aspect: When one thinks about it, almost all festivals were designed around the local harvest cycle for the community. So, Dussehra and Naveena Durga mark the planting of the winter crop, which commences right after Navdurga gets over. This takes about 20 days and, therefore, Diwali becomes the celebration at the end of the sowing season. Similarly, harvest festivals in other geographies and cultures follow a similar logic-flow.

2) The Health and Wellness aspect: It is argued that the cyclical nature of seasons is also designed to allow our physical and emotional health to nurture. In the post-monsoon phase of Shradhh, the body prepares itself for fasting, through gradual and selective abstinence. Then, the Navdurga period is marked by intermittent fasting and feasting, gradually moving into normal food, leading to the feasting of the festivities. And the emotional and spiritual body goes through the same process of preparation, abstinence, normalcy and an overwhelming smorgasbord of experiences.

3) The Social and Cultural aspect: Winter is the time for hibernation and reflection. Therefore, the festival season is a gradual build-up and phase down to the long wait. Beginning with the Shradhh, the month dedicated to paying tributes to the tribe and ancestor-worship. Once that debt is settled, Navdurga, a community celebration of feminine divinity, and Dussehra, signifying the victory of good over evil, follow. The grand finale of festivities with family, friends and business comes at Diwali. This falls just before we set in for winter hibernation, until the harvest is ripe for reaping at Makar Sankranthi in January, when the sun cycle turns.

This aspect of India is truly fascinating. Mark Twain reportedly said, 'India is the cradle of the human race, the birthplace of human speech, the mother of history, the grandmother of legend, and the great-grandmother of tradition. Our most valuable and most constructive materials in the history of man are treasured up in India only.'

Does this inspire you to think of any favourite festival stories or anecdotes that are rooted in rationality and science?

## TO THINK AND DO THIS WEEK

### THINK

Which is your favourite festival since childhood? Why?

### DO

Each day this week, perform one festivals-related ritual with your family. You can draw a rangoli, fly kites, perform aarti, light candles, exchange presents, dress up or burn effigies. Just have fun.

Experience:

Learnings:

Challenges:

WEEK 43

# GROUND YOURSELF FROM RADIATION

*'In my forties, I faced a dilemma:*
*Understand the biological effects of radiation*
*or die prematurely. I chose to understand radiation.'*

STEVEN MAGEE

## THE CONTEXT

This week's RedPill topic involves both science and (seemingly) magic. In a digital era wherein we have allowed cellphones to invade us, our enquiry is on how to GROUND YOURSELF FROM RADIATION. This topic is based on the original problem that Eika has been trying to solve – that of minimizing use of cellphones in our family.

## THE PROCESS

We came across varied information and opinions as we researched whitepapers written on the subject. All the data seemed to suggest a disturbing hypothesis—we have created this world of cellphone technology to make our lives convenient and easy. The same convenience, however, is also choking our emotional, intellectual and neural selves.

In a detailed conversation with our friend Ajay Poddar (founder of Environics), we learned that radiation from our mobile phones travels in regular sine waves that disturbs and interferes with our brain's neural signals that travel in regular random waves. Much like in an ECG. When this happens, and it happens every time that we are within the radiation reach of the mobile, the body-mind network undergoes stress, leading to physical and emotional detriment.

As a solution, Ajay has extensively researched and created an Environics chip that can be installed on all your electronic devices. Every animate and inanimate object has its own natural frequency radiation. This composition and the natural frequency of the Environics chip radiate in terra hertz in random waves, and carry the mobile phones' microwaves in random form. This, therefore, resonates with the body, thereby diffusing the effect of the mobile radiation.

We would not have believed it had Ajay not demonstrated with a simple resistance experiment with and without the mobile phone in the hand. The physical body resistance, and the mind-body connect simply breaks down the moment you hold a mobile phone in your hand. Your body, literally does not accept instruction from the mind.

In fact, these mobile radiation waves interfere with ALL body and mind functions – digestion, exercise, mental faculties and sleep. So be very careful where you keep your mobiles; they will have an impact on you.

## THE LEARNINGS

1) Keep any device that radiates electromagnetic waves as far away from yourself as possible. This involves taking simple steps like using headphones for speaking, no phones on dinner tables and in the bedroom, and so on.

2) Get your geopathic stress levels tested, both at home and your work and living spaces. We did this and have installed a certain number of Environics chips to mitigate the effects of possible radiation.
3) Be aware of, nurture, nourish and preserve the body's congruity and the mind-body connect. Meditation and self-awareness builds up that resilience.

**Note:** We are cognizant that this is a technical topic and there would be arguments for and against the radiation theories and practises discussed here. If your interest is piqued, please do your own research and form your independent views on this subject.

## TO THINK AND DO THIS WEEK

### THINK

Have you ever examined your surroundings to figure the kinds of radiation you are exposed to on a daily or hourly basis, even while you're asleep?

### DO

Try a 'Digital Detox'. No screens and devices this week, for two hours every day and from 8 p.m.–10 p.m., as a rule. Do this strictly, please. It's only for one week and you will see benefits.

Experience:

Learnings:

Challenges:

WEEK 44

# BIO-HACKING YOUR MIND AND BODY FOR PERFORMANCE

*'Rule your mind or it will rule you.'*

HORACE

## THE CONTEXT

Eika and I have been deeply fascinated with the mind and body connection and this week's enquiry around BIO-HACKING THE MIND AND BODY FOR OPTIMAL PERFORMANCE became extra interesting when we tried deep immersion with our expert friend, Shayamal Vallabhjee.

## THE PROCESS

This week is all about quality time spent with Shayamal to understand this subject. Let's begin with his introduction. Shayamal is a South African sports scientist, psychologist, bio-hacker and entrepreneur with two decades of experience in high-performance sport. A former monk with ISKCON, he has authored four books, and is reputed as a TEDx speaker, an INK Talks & Australia India Youth Fellow, *Men's Health* 'Trainer of the Year 2014', a global fitness advisory board member at Herbalife, and organising committee member of the United Nations Global Change Makers Conference. He has worked with institutions such as the South African and Indian cricket and Davis Cup teams, Kings XI Punjab, Kenyan Athletics Team, ATP Tour, Oprah Winfrey Leadership Academy for Girls, and more. Phew!

And we are collaborating with him to ensure we spread the idea of bio-hacking in order to optimize human performance.

As a scientist, Shayamal believes his role is not to answer questions, but, in fact, to question the answers. It is this life philosophy, combined with his obsession with human physiology and psyche, which makes him one of the world's leading experts in sports science.

'I work in a world where the margin for error is miniscule and the penalty for failure is very high,' says Shayamal. 'In a world where the difference between gold and silver is less than 0.1 per cent, my job is to decode the science and re-program an athletes limiting beliefs, all in an effort to truly optimize human potential. Sometimes, the best place to test anything is on yourself.'

As a result, over the last year, he has been doing less training mileage but running faster in races, eating more and losing weight, sleeping optimally, waking up fully recovered, thinking clearer and operating far more productively than he has done in the last 20 years. The question is how? And can we all do this?

## THE LEARNINGS

If you want to hack your body and mind, here is a good place to start. These are some of Shayamal's easier bio-hacks. 'I've summedf up a list of the most cost-effective hacks that will yield the quickest results. I am only scratching the surface here. As you can imagine, this list is endless and can become an interesting discussion by itself.'

The following are Shayamal's words of advice.

1) **Understand Your Strengths:** In the world of sport, I optimize human performance by leveraging an individual's strengths, and we define 'strength' as a skill that gives you a competitive advantage in a high-performing environment. If you can achieve material success by leveraging a talent or skill, imagine what you could do to your body if you knew its internal strengths. Start by taking simple tests: allergy, intolerance, genetics and gut micro-biome tests. These will give you a blueprint of your body's physiological strengths. All you need to do then is follow the breadcrumbs on your path to success. Modify your food in accordance with your allergy and intolerance results, and then map these with your gut micro-biome cultures. Modify your training based on your genetic disposition. You will start to yield results faster than you could imagine because for the first time in your life, you will be working with your body and not against it.

2) **Cold Showers:** Most of the world's mental health issues (depression, anxiety, lack of focus, autoimmune brain disorders, early onset Alzheimer's etc.) are all directly correlated to a Leaky Brain Syndrome, a condition in which the integrity of the blood-brain barrier is compromised. Daily cold showers and ice baths help maintain the integrity of this barrier. Ice baths have been used traditionally in Eastern Europe and Japanese cultures for ages. Cold Immersion Therapy also reduces the body's

inflammation response and can metabolise fat cells faster than any training modality. If you want to live longer and healthy, there are only two things you need to do: reduce your body's response to inflammation and control your body's glycaemic variability. Ice baths take care of the first one better than any other prescription.

I use a hot/cold contrast shower that stimulates the blood-brain barrier and brings about micro healing to muscles.

(30 seconds of cold water + 10 seconds of hot Water) x 10 sets.

I end with one minute of cold immersion. This is my personal shower routine.

3) **Breath Work:** Our breath is the most important tool we have at our disposal. Unfortunately, it is the one aspect of our physiology we take most for granted. The simple science of breathing is that the longer the inhalation, the more rejuvenated and invigorated you will feel; and the longer the exhalation, the more relaxed you will feel. Your breath controls your sympathetic and parasympathetic nervous systems, which regulate your entire endocrine system (hormones). You can literally detoxify and heal your body with your breath. Sadly, more than 90 per cent of the world does chest breathing (which is a shallow breathe). With chest breathing, you do not utilize the full capacity of your lung. To train oneself to do deep-belly breathing, I have come up with a simple hack. Tie a light piece of elastic string around your belly, in line with your navel. (You can wear this under your shirt). Throughout the day, take your awareness to that elastic string. If you can feel it expand and contract with your breath, it is an

indication that you are belly breathing and using more of your lung capacity. Moving your awareness to the string is also a fantastic form of meditation.

4) **Optimize Your Sleep:** Quality sleep is fast becoming the most elusive component in an individual's life. In my world, sleep is the most important recovery tool in our arsenal and it's imperative that we attempt to maximize it. In fact, poor quality sleep triggers cortisol, which puts your body in a stress-response mode. It's the number one reason why you put on weight and struggle to have quality relationships. In order to get a restful night's sleep, everyone needs at least 10 per cent of their sleep time to be in REM and the Deep Sleep Zone. Most people get less than 4 per cent, which means you have not recovered, you are stressed and, most importantly, are functioning well below your optimum potential. If you want to optimize your sleep, this is my routine:
   - *Cold showers at night*: This brings down the body's core temperature and promotes better sleep.
   - *No digital devices two hours before bed*: White, yellow and blue lights decrease the production of melatonin in the brain. This is why you struggle to fall asleep.
   - Try to wake up at the same time and in alignment with the rising sun. This helps regulate your circadian rhythm with the optimal functioning of the human body.
   - *Keep a red lamp in your bedroom*: Switch this on 45 minutes before you sleep. Red light increases your response to Deep and REM sleep.
   - Keep the temperature of the room at 19 degrees Celsius and the humidity at 50 per cent. These are the most optimal conditions for the promotion of quality sleep.

5) **Use Caffeine as a Carrier:** Caffeine is a powerful compound and one that can bypass the blood-brain barrier. This is the reason why most people are buzzing 45 minutes after a coffee shot (this depends on an individual's caffeine sensitivity, as well). I use caffeine as a carrier of amino acids into the brain. One such amino acid is theanine – an extract found in tea that helps balance the neurotransmitters in your brain. Theanine has been associated with enhanced cognitive performance, promotes relaxation, and improves sleep quality and weight loss in certain studies. Two for my favourite hacks with caffeine are:
   - Add 100mg of theanine powder to your morning coffee. No sugar or lactose milk.
   - Have an espresso shot when you want to take a nap. Caffeine takes 45 minutes to hit the blood stream and activate the hormones in your brain. If you have it just before you sleep, you will doze off and wake up fully charged in 25–35 minutes.

6) **Upgrade Your Meditation:** This is the fastest growing skill helping people de-stress and rejuvenate. Unfortunately, if you not a regular meditator, it is going to take you a long time to unlock these benefits. Using brainwave tracks like theta waves or binaural beats will enhance the quality of your meditation. These waves help transition you into a deep-relaxation state and activate your subconscious pathways in just a few minutes. This is a brilliant way to enhance creativity and focus.

## TO THINK AND DO THIS WEEK

### THINK

How comfortable are you experimenting with anything? How far would you go to experiment with your body?

### DO

Experiment with the lung capacity thread under your shirt this week. And with the alternating hot and cold shower routine (as described in this chapter). Assess the difference you feel.

Experience:

Learnings:

Challenges:

# WEEK 45

# COLLABORATIONS AS A CREATIVITY TURBOCHARGER

*'Music gives a soul to the Universe,*
*wings to the mind, flight to the imagination, a charm to sadness,*
*gaiety and life to everything.'*

PLATO

## THE CONTEXT

Eika has always been an ardent music buff, while I get excited about sources of creativity. So this week's RedPill was about COLLABORATIONS AS A CREATIVITY TURBOCHARGER. While Eika and I have collaborated with multiple organizations and people in our corporate life, our immediate trigger to discuss and deep dive into this topic was due to our recent friendship with this amazing couple who form the band, Maati Baani.

## THE PROCESS

Nirali and Kartik Shah are the musical genius couple who formed Maati Baani to bring out Indian folk music and other Indian sounds to the world. The duo have performed across the world (most recently in Ibiza and Berlin), shared their experience on sundry TEDx and INK platforms, and are now experts in spotting talent and creating fabulous collaborations across India and the world. Eika and I were fortunate to have a deep immersion on the subject, spending time with our young friends at their studio and then over a breakfast at our home.

What completely blew our mind about this musical duo is the amazing number of multi-country, multi-cultural global collaborations of which they have been a part, and the process they have developed to streamline their global collaboration timelines from nine months (Heal the world) to 25 days (We are the champions), as they refined their learnings. It has been truly inspirational for us.

## THE LEARNINGS

As Kartik articulated, all Maati Baani collaborations should consist of three things – a bigger purpose, connecting cultures and creating new experiences and opportunities for diverse artists, and taking up new challenges and stretching the limits for music.

Why should you collaborate?

1) The collaboration process enriches you beyond your imagination by stretching the limits of your craft (irrespective of one's field)
2) This process allows you to experience the world in a different light and is quite easy in today's world of WhatsApp and Instagram, which allow for fluid communication and low-cost discoverability. Kartik spoke passionately about Iran, China and Indonesia as places to discover child prodigies in the field of music.

3) Finally, at a macro-level, collaboration allows fresh, unique talent to be discovered, since mass-entertainment platforms mainly present select (proven) artists.

And the secret sauce for success in Maati Baani's remote music collaborations:

- Select ideas for collaboration that give you goosebumps. You'll know then that you, at least, have a good starting point.
- Create and map a process that you can hone over time. Adhere to the process with discipline.
- Execute with a focus on quality. Do not accept less-than-excellent work from global collaborators and ensure that everybody is at the same quality levels. This focus on quality shows and attracts both your audience, as well as future global collaborators.

**RESOURCES**

Two interesting Maati Baani Collaboration links as below:

Heal the World (MJ Tribute)
https://youtu.be/h6d6Yo3DwVI

Balma
https://youtu.be/PspcQLrWGTI

If you enjoy their thoughts and music, do subscribe to Maati Baani's YouTube Channel and reach out to them.

## TO THINK AND DO THIS WEEK

### THINK

Competition versus Collaboration: What do you think?

### DO

Figure out a field you think you know something about, reach out to an expert in that field, and propose a collaborative project that gives you goosebumps.

Experience:

Learnings:

Challenges:

WEEK 46

# INDIAN MANAGEMENT, THE NEW SUPERPOWER

*'India conquered and dominated China culturally for 20 centuries without ever having to send a single soldier across her border.'*

HU SHIH

## THE CONTEXT

As a mythologist, Eika has been a passionate evangelist of India's ancient wisdom as a source of soft power. And I have been influenced to ruminate about the rise of India globally as a soft power by listening to Shashi Tharoor's compelling TED talk on this topic, where he argues how Bollywood, curries and Indian thought (amongst others) is powerfully influencing foreign cultures and raising our stature across the world. Hence, this week's RedPill – INDIAN MANAGEMENT, THE NEW SUPERPOWER.

## THE PROCESS

The topic encouraged us to recap some of our on-going conversations and start fresh discussions around a legendary book launch I attended last weekend. Legendary, because I got to listen in and absorb learnings from the famed RG – R. Gopalakrishnan (ex-vice chairman at HLL and ex-director at Tata Sons) and author of the book, *The Made In India Manager* (co-authored with Ranjan Banerjee, Dean at SP Jain Institute of Management and Research).

R. Gopalakrishnan's thesis is simple and powerful as a good insight. There is a secret recipe that makes Indian managers the toast of the global business and academic world. Some of the famous names in this category are Indra Nooyi, Sundar Pichai, Satya Nadella, Rakesh Kapoor, Ajay Banga, Atul Sarin et al.

## THE LEARNINGS

While the above book neatly details the rationale for the thesis, here are five key nuggets and action points it proposes:

1) 'Growing up in India is an extraordinary preparation for management,' once said C. K. Prahalad, professor of corporate strategy at the University of Michigan. Combine this statement with a 2011 Egon Zehneder study of S&P 500 CEOs, which found that Indians led more S&P 500 companies than people of any other nationality, apart from Americans. And the tribe has only expanded since with more tech companies and academic institutions being helmed by 'made-in-India' managers. So, we have strong tailwinds if we want to leverage ourselves on the global stage.

2) Indian managers perform well on both vectors of management – the thinking or the intellectual vector, and

the action or the transactional vector. The reason for this is a secret recipe, which according to the two authors, has four unique ingredients:

- Growing up in a crushingly competitive, highly aspirational environment.
- Exposure to extraordinary setbacks that accelerate personal learning.
- The ability to work hard along with intuitive adaptability and creativity.
- The capability to think in English (but act in a local or vernacular manner).

When one considers these four ingredients, typically Indian adaptations such as *jugaad*, missed call, Hinglish and RAC seats come into play, which seek to overcome the resource-constrained environments most Indians face every day of their lives. Hence, Indian managers have the intrinsic DNA to 'do more with less'.

3) India is a colloidal society, which allows Indians to live and breathe and navigate diversity at every stage. Since 'colloids work on nature's principle of soft equilibrium- networking, diversity, redundancy, collaboration and adaptation', Made-in-India managers develop skills to adeptly and calmly navigate multi-cultural environments. Of course, one of the bolt-on skills needed for these managers is empathy, which, as Nadella says in his book *Reboot*, can be imbibed or dialled-up via life's circumstances.

4) The influence of one's family is immense. Since management is about delivery via people, our family unit's aspirations and desires, the nurturing by an elder figure like a grandparent

or an uncle prepare the Made-in-India manager well for the post VUCA world – now called BOCA (Blurred boundaries, work Overload, increased Complexity, and Addiction to technology). No wonder then, according to the research of the authors, Made-In-India managers credit their family members as their idols and role models much more than managers of other nationalities.

5) Looking beyond 100 years of Anglo–American MBA thoughts. While we have all imbibed the Harvard–Stanford diets of management thought, there is merit in reading some of our own brilliant Indian texts like the *Bhagwad Gita*, the *Arthashastra* and the *Mahabharata* ('If it has ever happened, it is in the *Mahabharata*'). The concepts of servant leadership, mindfulness and societal good etc. are all here, as are inspirations for cross-discipline learnings and self-mastery.

**Note:** If you have young children, the *Amar Chitra Katha* series is a GREAT start.

**RESOURCES**

- *Imagining India: Ideas for the New Century* by Nandan Nilekani
- Below is an article that Eika recently published about the post-VUCA world.

  How many of these trends do you agree with?

### From VUCA to the SELF

In today's chaotic world, I submit to you that at the other end of Volatility, Uncertainty, Complexity and Ambiguity (VUCA) are Simplicity and Experiential Life in Freedom (SELF)

There has been much conversation and emotion, stress and heartburn, and almost panic and fear about the VUCA that surrounds, engulfs and threatens to drown us everyday, at work and at home, as professionals, spouses, parents and as humans on the treadmill of a planet.

Well, here's the good news. There is a world at the other end of the tumult ... and, when the dust settles, it is definitely a changed world from the one we took off from – a world more serene, humane and harmonious. New realities will emerge, and some myths would have been busted.

Here's crystal-gazing at ten myths that will have exploded by the end of the next decade:

1. The Myth of House of Brands Material Luxury: makes niche forages into the cottage industry of sustainable Boutique Handcrafted Story.
2. The Myth of Money as currency: becomes the relationship with Circular Economy Barters.
3. The Myth of Asset Ownership: replaced by Co-Sharing and The Gig Economy.
4. The Myth of the Global Large Corporation: learns from Block Chain to become organized in Locally Distributed Ledgers.
5. The Myth of Career: inverts the funnel to tasks, jobs, passion projects and super-temps – the quintessential Plug-n-Play Professional.

6. The Myth of Networking: replicates AI to plug into Intuition-linked Super-Connecting.
7. The Myth of the General Generalist: the Jack-of-Some-Trades makes space for either the Super Functionalist or the Super Join-the-Dots Generalist.
8. The Myth of Conspicuous Consumption: shifts with awareness into Conscious Consummation.
9. The Myth of Competition: leverages commoditization of information to processing based Strength-Led-Collaboration and Co-Creation.
10. The Myth of Polar Binaries: the starkness of black & white, this & that, day & night, male & female flows into the fluidity of the Continuum/Spectrum of colourful, grey, timelessness, gender – Infinite Possibilities – from the Byte to the Qubit.

And, therefore, to survive, cope and heal will be a function of the truest, the most centred, the super-authentic version of our own Self that we can possibly be. As the millennials and Gen-Z rapidly step into their well-deserved and completely naturalised leadership roles, it will be the present–day leadership, bred on a diet of the Global Financial Crisis (GFC) and VUCA that will struggle with control and careers, with heads and hierarchies, with money and material. Unless they prepare now – they Unlearn, Re-learn, and Hyper learn, and move into the Simplicity and Experiential Life in Freedom (SELF).

One of the ways to do that would be to embrace the philosophy of 52RedPills.

## TO THINK AND DO THIS WEEK

### THINK

What's your view on the post-VUCA world? How prepared are you for it?

### DO

Do your own 360-degree appraisal this week, both personal and professional. Call or meet your parent, boss, manager, child, subordinate, spouse, significant other, sibling, peer or colleague. (Note: Any of these relationships can be from the past or the present.) Ask them about your greatest strength, and what they think holds you back from your greatness.

Experience:

Learnings:

Challenges:

WEEK 47

# DECODING HOMEOPATHY

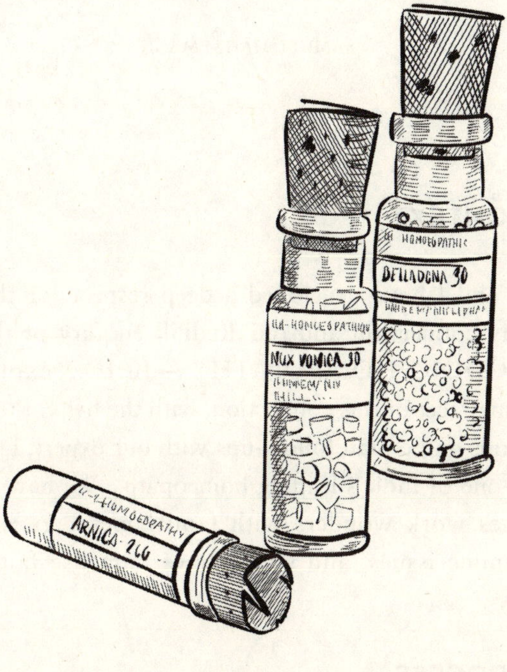

*'The highest ideal of cure is the speedy, gentle,*
*and enduring restoration of health*
*by the most trustworthy and least harmful way.'*

SAMUEL HAHNEMANN

## THE CONTEXT

Eika and I have developed a deep respect for the mind-body connection and our RedPill enquiry of this week – DECODING HOMEOPATHY – further explored an interesting facet of this connection, with the help of telephonic discussions and e-mail follow-ups with our expert, Dr Chetna Shukla, one of India's leading homeopaths. We have seen her medicines work wonders with family members who have autoimmune issues, and so we have immense faith in her abilities.

## THE PROCESS

With the conversation increasingly leaning towards holistic living, it makes sense to understand homeopathy in greater detail, beyond the 'sweet placebo pill' perception generally held about this area of medicine. We did our secondary research and spent an afternoon in deep discussion with Dr Shukla to understand her perspective on the rationale of homeopathy.

## THE LEARNINGS

First, the basics: Homeopathy is derived from the Greek words *homoios*, which means 'like' and *pathos*, which means 'suffering'. This indicates the basic premise of this science.

Dr Samuel Hahnemann, MD from the University of Erlangen, is regarded as the father of homeopathy with his famous treatise that was published in 1796.

In essence, consider the trinity of homeopathy:

- Law of Similars (like cures like) calls for individualization; exploring which medicine best resonates with an individual.
- Law of Singular Medicine
- Law of Minimum Dosage of Medicine (dilutions)

Homeopathy is *nanopharmacology* at its best.

While Western medicine is dependent on the Law of Contraria and Physical Doses, homoeopathy finds its foundation in the Law of Similars and the Law of Minimum Dosage.

Benefits of Homeopathy:

1. Efficient medicine
2. Singular medicine
3. Safe and effective
4. Genuine
5. Natural medicine

Now, here is the difficult part – the mind-bending theoretical foundation of Homeopathy in three points with actionable takeaways:

1) **Science accepts one fact:** All cells in human (all animals too) body tissues are electrically polarized. In other words, they maintain a voltage difference across the cell's plasma membrane, known as the membrane potential. Action potentials are generated by special types of voltage-gated-ion channels embedded in a cell's plasma membrane. This is the only tangible aspect of the energetic existence of an animal body. This electrical potential is the interphase between the material existence and the energetic and spiritual existence of the human body. Beyond this, the energetic aspect of human body is immaterial and intangible. This intangible and immaterial *animating* energy is termed simply as the Vital Force in homoeopathy.

   **Note:** *This part of the discussion reminded us of the famous Star Wars line: 'May the force be with you.'*

   **Action:** In physical health terms, understanding your blood markers is important. For every annual medical health check report you get, put in a visit to a homeopath to get additional insights about the internal state of your body.

2) In the above 'energy model', let us remember that each cell in the animal body has electricity. The whole human body is electrically charged; it is now akin to a battery. This electric system has its own anatomy and physiology that is independent of the anatomy and physiology of the

material and tangible body. The energy anatomy is the popular seven-*chakra* system and the energy meridians. This electrical energy of the entire human body creates a 'field' that is very forceful. Everyone has their own unique energy field, their signature energy pattern. These energy fields are like fingerprints; just as no two individuals can have the same fingerprints, no two individuals can have the same signature energy pattern. This field is a circuit and also a conduit that attracts and or repels other energetic fields! Emotions constitute the physiology of this electrically charged human.

**Action:** The reason why a homeopath asks numerous probing questions on one's disposition, temperament, dreams, relationships, state of mind and emotions is to establish and reveal the deep mind–body connection. This allows them to establish a link between the disharmony in the mind that is relayed in the body as disease. The answers also aid the homeopath in individualizing the person with the disease and, thereafter, choosing the 'similar' medicine that has in its repertory a similar disease matrix. The homoeopath then prepares the relevant mini-dosages required for 'overall' harmony of the patient. Emotional well being and balance is a major positive outcome for this science. Hence, increase your self-awareness about your mind and body as a useful exercise; it might be useful for you to understand your interconnectedness, with or without a visit to the homeopath.

3) **The Body–Food Connection:** The superconductor activity of food takes place at the quantum level of the human

body. This quantum working is orchestrated by the Vital Force. The Vital Force helps the organism utilize the foods vitality to nourish the body, the psyche and the spirit. However, in the last few decades, the food we consume is disconnected from nature (due to insecticides and pesticides). In recent times, human science has tampered with the basics of most foods (especially animal proteins and now the new introduction of genetically modified foods) and made unauthorized alterations to its dynamics. The consumption of chemically laden and genetically modified foods is responsible for the deterioration of the human organism in the body and psyche. Foods that are unaltered and remain closer to their natural state contain more of the earth's intelligence and will be better utilized to nourish the body and psyche that is in alignment with nature and our higher purpose.

**Action:** The popular phrase 'you are what you eat' has never been truer. Hence, go raw and organic as much as possible as 'you become what you eat'. Some useful tips in RedPill indicated the addition of animal foods and plants (vegetables) in your diet will be a key recommendation from a homeopath.

**Note:** The above material is attributed to Dr Chetna Shukla's research, which she generously shared with us. The takeaways and nuggets are ours and not intended as expert medical comments, but as thought starters.

## TO THINK AND DO THIS WEEK

### THINK

What do you believe or think about alternative medical practices that are alternatives to allopathy? Which ones do you know about? And what do you know about them?

________________________________________

________________________________________

### DO

This week is about living in awareness of the mind-body connect. So, be aware of every breath, emotion, action, word and thought. And study the effect it has on your body (and vice versa). When your body is hungry, what's your mind thinking? When you're stressed, how is your body feeling, and so on? Document yourself physically, intellectually and emotionally this week.

________________________________________

________________________________________

Experience:

________________________________________

________________________________________

Learnings:

________________________________________

________________________________________

Challenges:

________________________________________

________________________________________

WEEK 48

# PERSONAL BHAGS

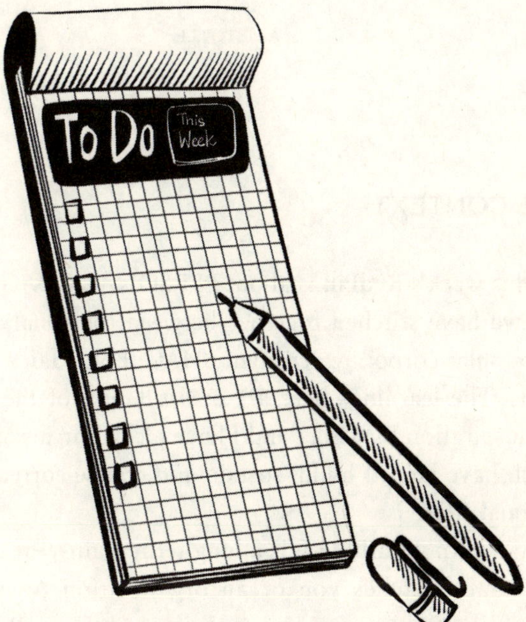

*'We are what we repeatedly do.*
*Excellence, then, is not an act, but a habit.'*

ARISTOTLE

## THE CONTEXT

This week's RedPill is about PERSONAL BHAGs, a phrase we have stitched together between (personal) goals and the popular corporate acronym BHAG: Bold Hairy Audacious Goals. The learnings here are a distillation of the principles and inspiration that Eika and I have picked up across the year, which have helped build, sustain and course-correct our own personal BHAGs.

As we know, a BHAG is a long-term multi-year compelling goal that stretches you or an organization towards some compelling outcome. Jim Collins and Jerry Porras first coined the term BHAG (pronounced BEE-hag) in their iconic 1994 book, *Built To Last: Successful Habits of Visionary Companies*, and it has inspired us ever since we read it.

We also read in an article that a brave BHAG should have a 'gulp factor', implying that when people initially hear about it, they swallow hard to absorb it. Fabulous sentiment!

While everybody has goals and bucket lists, we would like to assert that personal BHAGs are simply 'Goals on Steroids' – personal objectives that have stretch and ambition built into them. Every few years, we make a five-year-plan, full of personal BHAGs and, miraculously, we achieve a lot of them. It's almost like the *kayanaat* (universe) is conspiring to act upon our goals (said with a hat-tip to SRK in the Bollywood movie, *Om Shanti Om*)

## THE PROCESS

We loved the life story of Paul Brown, one of the world's foremost applied neuroscientists, academic and author. Eika met him in London this week. Paul's personal BHAG has been to reverse his ageing. When he turned 70, he made a series of choices to power this goal to make him live healthy and happy till the age of 80. Now that he has crossed 80 comfortably, his personal BHAG on ageing has gone up to 93.5 years. Why 93.5? He has an esoteric probability-based life expectancy calculation to explain that! Eika will be working with him on a RedPill project sometime in the future, so hopefully, we will observe (and learn from) the progress of this ambitious goal.

What makes a personal BHAG and why is it important?

It is important if one believes that our lives have purpose, and that we all have the ability to tap into our individual potential and be our best selves. Eika now has a (soon to be patented) leadership model for this, so we are believers in this journey all the way.

## THE LEARNINGS

A personal BHAG should have three critical elements. As MBAs, Eika and I have made a simple ABC for the this formula:

- Ambition (Stretch)
- Belief (Perseverance)
- Contribution (Useful to the world)

Occasionally, there will be failures and setbacks, but the trick is to keep the faith and continue to 'walk through hell with a smile'. We had a tough fortnight and one of the inspirations we kept using for positive self-talk is the famous Amitabh Bachchan interview where he quotes his father's advice on life and its vicissitudes:

> *Mann ka ho, woh accha,*
> *Na ho, toh aur bhi accha.*

Essentially saying that there is a divine strength in each one of us, which we need to acknowledge and tap into. (This is science articulated a little as pop psychology, but the proof is that positive self-talk absolutely works.) We have tried this, in times of challenges, and benefited from the exercise.

Eika and I have our own personal BHAGs and they provide energy and purpose to our lives. And we share them with each other to hold each other accountable for working towards them on a daily basis.

We encourage YOU to think about your own personal BHAGs.

## RESOURCES

- *Built To Last: Successful Habits of Visionary Companies* by Jim Collins and Jerry Porras
- Check out books on 'Building a Vision Board' on Amazon and create one for yourself.

## TO THINK AND DO THIS WEEK

### THINK

What's your most ambitious or fantastical version of yourself?

### DO

Make your own vision board, with at least five 'visions'. Then, list down what you need to do TODAY to get those to come true.

Experience:

Learnings:

Challenges:

WEEK 49

# SERENDIPITY AND PASSION

*'What you seek is seeking you.'*

RUMI

## THE CONTEXT

Eika and I have been lifelong believers in serendipity and this week's RedPill combines that belief with passion. And so, our enquiry is SERENDIPITY AND PASSION. Our provocation is that just like a life unexamined is not worth living, similarly, a life without nurturing a passion is a purposeless life.

> **Fun exercise:** Look up the fascinating origin of the word serendipity.

The recent demise of reputed ad-film maker and theatre personality Alyque Padamsee reminded us of a man who nurtured a love and passion for the performing arts, while being one of the pioneers of Indian advertising. Eika and I have nurtured our passions, also – Eika is a mythologist by passion, as well as a full-time CEO; and I am a public-speaking evangelist, while pursuing a career in consumer-facing technology. In these multiple roles across the years of our corporate career, serendipity has played a great role in us stumbling upon opportunities or developing connections with like-minded people.

## THE PROCESS

Our recent inspiration for this premise has been one of Eika's earliest friends from school, Nitin Shrestha, who researches, restores and curates beautiful objects – from Vespa scooter to HMV gramophones, and from antique clocks to princely heirlooms. We spoke to him regarding the process by which he literally turns junk into treasure, and how this 25-years-long passion has taught him life lessons and given him purpose.

## THE LEARNINGS

1) Nurturing a passion develops a life-long discipline, which is as true for Nitin as it is for us. The practice of scavenging for treasures in *chor bazaars*, developing an art of negotiation to get a sense of pricing, building a network of like-minded collectors and curators – all of this takes perseverance and builds discipline for Nitin. Similarly, the act of co-authoring a book (*Speechless*, in my case) took 18 months and extreme discipline to get it completed, sharpened and polished before eventual publishing. As they say, it takes ten years to become an overnight sensation.

2) Nurturing a passion makes you more open to the world and its possibilities. And that is where serendipity comes in. Nitin spoke to us about recently finding the original packaging of an artefact that he had carefully collected and

stowed away, almost 20 years ago. Eika and I have wanted to take a couple of actions for our passions and serendipity has ensured help (magically), including the right people meeting us at the appropriate times. Pop psychology: When you are more open to the world, a lot of stuff starts coming your way.

3) Following a passion allows you to increase your natural curiosity and become more aware and knowledgeable about your world, history and heritage, as well as the arts and sciences. This makes one more interesting as a person (something that our good friend Virginia Sharma, Director marketing Solutions for LinkedIn strongly espouses). Today, Eika is one of the foremost voices on mythology in India, having established the country's first mythology festival, Aakhayan, and she is currently penning a book for corporate women using our ancient knowledge. Think of this as India's version to Sheryl Sandberg's *Lean In*.

Bonus Tip from our super-curator, Nitin: Some of the better-known places for finding interesting antiques are Radha Bazaar and Malik Bazaar in Kolkata, and the chor bazaars of Old Delhi and Mumbai. (But only if you know your wares, so caveat emptor.)

**Golden Question:** What passions have you nurtured? What has enabled or stopped you in following and nurturing your passion? And, more importantly, can your passion become your profession?

## RESOURCES

- *Thrive: The Third Metric to Redefining Success and Creating a Life of Well-Being, Wisdom, and Wonder* by Arianna Huffington
- Lonely Planet Guides for travel
- *The Winning Way 2.0: Learnings From Sport for Managers* by Anita Bhogle and Harsha Bhogle
- *The Power of Moments* by Chip Heath and Dan Heath
- *A Double Life: My Exciting Years in Theater and Advertising* by Alyque Padamsee (with Arun Prabhu)

## TO THINK AND DO THIS WEEK

### THINK

Which passions (if any) have you lost along the way? Which of these do you miss?

____________________________________________

____________________________________________

____________________________________________

### DO

Explore your city/town. Walk through old lanes and bylanes, navigate via little shops and nooks, peek into little warehouses and tucked away inns and restaurants, amble through monuments and museums, discover hidden treasures troves and see which of them ignites a long-lost hidden passion.

____________________________________________

____________________________________________

Experience:

____________________________________________

____________________________________________

Learnings:

____________________________________________

____________________________________________

Challenges:

____________________________________________

____________________________________________

WEEK 50

# THINKING MACRO

*'The past was no fun.'*

YUVAL NOAH HARARI

## THE CONTEXT

The buzz and excitement in the Banerjee household this week was around Yuval Noah Harari's ideas. Given the expansive worldview of this renowned historian, bestselling author and futurist, the RedPill topic is THINKING MACRO!

## THE PROCESS

Eika and I were privileged to listen to Professor Harari (Eika, to her great delight, managed to ask him an audience question, also) at the annual lecture event. We are massive fans of his mind-bending books, *Sapiens* and *Homo Deus*. Most of the evening's conversations revolved around his just-released third book, *21 Lessons for the 21st Century*. Harari's thinking is fascinating as he connects data and events at a Meta level and paints plausible (including dystopian) glimpses into the future of humankind.

Harari's three key nuggets for thinking about the world at a macro level:

1) Mankind has achieved three major things in the 20th century:
   a) Overcome Famine: For the first time in human history, more people die of diseases related to (bad) eating than starvation.
   b) Overcome Plague: There are no large-scale plagues wiping off millions in this century.
   c) Overcome War: With the dramatic reduction of war, more people die of road accidents annually than in all wars combined across the world. (According to an interesting perspective shared by Harari, sugar kills more people globally than gunpowder!)

2) Challenges of the 21st century:
   a) Return of War (especially a Nuclear one): As Harari says drily, 'Never underestimate human stupidity.'
   b) Ecological Collapse: Global collaborations, as well as new and practical eco-friendly technologies are needed to avoid this.
   c) Technological Disruption: Technology is slowly yet surely upgrading humans into (irresponsible) Gods. For the first time, humans have gone beyond manipulating the world around us to manipulating the world *inside* us via genetic engineering and bio-wearables based on IoT (Internet of Things). Soon, natural selection will be replaced by intelligent design, bringing the power versus wisdom debate into focus.

3) As a result of the above transformations, Harari cautioned about three risks in the 21st century:
   a) The Rise of the Useless Class: Automation and AI will take away a lot of jobs, and the workforce will continuously need to upgrade skills else risk becoming 'useless'.
   b) The Emergence of Digital Dictatorships: Some countries could transform into Orwellian 'Big Brother' states, while other countries could turn into neo-colonists and harvest data colonies, thereby, forcing poorer countries to come together and form cartels and (data) trade blocs.
   c) Interdependence of Countries: Global challenges will demand global solutions. Suddenly, no nation will be completely independent, and challenges like global warming and human cloning will only be sustainably handled with all countries aligning together.

These learnings provided an impetus for us to understand the global issues facing us today in greater detail since they are all interrelated. One of the immediate actions we took was to pick up online subscriptions to two global newspapers that provide analytical editorial content and OpEds.

**RESOURCES**

- *Sapiens*, *Homo Deus* and *21 Lessons for the 21st Century* by Yuval Noah Harari
- *Factfulness: Ten Reasons We're Wrong About The World - And Why Things Are Better Than You Think* by Hans Rosling, Anna Rosling and Ola Rosling.

## TO THINK AND DO THIS WEEK

### THINK

What is the larger impact of your work? On your organization, society and the environment? What is the impact of your life on all of these?

___

___

___

### DO

Predict the future of your favourite three industries this week. Meet people working in those industries to figure their preparedness for the future.

___

___

___

Experience:

___

___

Learnings:

___

___

Challenges:

___

___

WEEK 51

# THE JOY OF COFFEE

*'Coffee, the favourite drink of the civilised world.'*

THOMAS JEFFERSON

## THE CONTEXT

Merry Christmas, folks! The festive season is here. Eika and I will be spending some quality time with family and friends, with coffee and conversations taking centre stage. As a toast and testament, this week's RedPill is on THE JOY OF COFFEE.

## THE PROCESS

Over the course of this year, we have imbibed this beverage across various avatars, filter coffee in Tamil Nadu, Nespresso capsules in Europe, kopi luwak in Indonesia, and so on; and in different settings, Di Bella, Blue Tokai, Kiononia Coffee Roasters, etc. Our RedPill journey this week was made special by a dedicated coffee journey at a premium coffee chain, led by a well-known Coffee Master and national winner of a prestigious Barista Championship.

## THE LEARNINGS

- The history and geography of coffee is fascinating. The apocryphal origin of coffee around 800 AD in Ethiopia by the Sufi goatherd Kaldi is an oft-told story.

- As part of our coffee journey, we tried various coffee blends across Ethiopia, India and Indonesia (Sumatra) brewed by a variety of methods – cold brew, pour over (my favourite, given the delicate use of a thin-spout kettle and filter paper), espresso and French press (for a bolder, richer brew). Note: Two other methods we heard about were siphon and chemex. Traditionally a tea drinker, Eika fell in love with the nitro cold brew, recently launched in Mumbai and other cities.

- We then tried Coffee Tasting, which works on the same rationale as whiskey or wine appreciation. It involved four steps – smell, slurp, locate and describe – as we judged the coffees on their aroma, acidity, body and flavour. While coffee never expires, we learned about the enemies of coffee from our Coffee Master, oxygen, heat, sunlight and moisture. We were taken through the roasting process, the countries of the coffee belt (between the Tropic of Cancer and the Tropic of Capricorn), and the process by which premium coffee chains buys some of the world's finest Arabica coffees.

- Our Coffee Master walked us through a little more theory regarding the three kinds of processes to remove the bean from the coffee seed, wet wash, dry wash and semi wash. We then had a delightful discussion on how a premium coffee chain ensures great care to live up to the four fundamentals of brewing a great cup of coffee:

1) Proportion
2) Grind
3) Water
4) Freshness

All this certainly made us respect the barista a bit more for making us their handcrafted beverages. And it has set me on the journey to become a certified Coffee Master in 2020.

Where did you have your best cup of coffee? Recall the memories associated with your favourite places for coffee.

## RESOURCES

A must-read book for coffee lovers: *Pour Your Heart Into It: How Starbucks Built a Company One Cup at a Time* by Howard Schultz. It brings alive the story of Starbucks and provides context to their mission statement, 'To inspire and nurture the human spirit – one cup, one person, and one neighbourhood at a time.'

## TO THINK AND DO THIS WEEK

### THINK

What does coffee (or tea, whiskey, beer or anything else that is your go-to drink) really mean to you?

________________________________________

________________________________________

### DO

Visit your favourite cafes or coffee shops this week, and order their signature drink at that place.

________________________________________

________________________________________

Experience:

________________________________________

________________________________________

Learnings:

________________________________________

________________________________________

Challenges:

________________________________________

________________________________________

### BONUS

Do this with different sets of friends and/or family, and you'll have multiplied your collective fun, too. You can also include pubs, bars and watering holes and try their signature creations.

________________________________________

WEEK 52

# REFLECT AND TURBOCHARGE

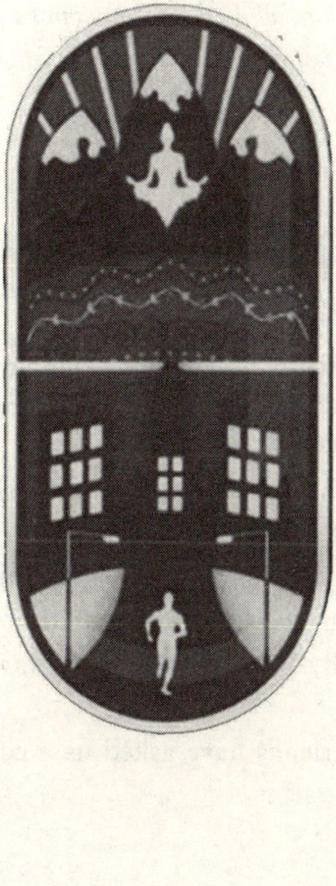

*'The heights by great men reached and kept*
*Were not attained in sudden flight,*
*But they, while their companions slept,*
*Were toiling upwards in the night.'*

HENRY LONGFELLOW

The 52RedPills journey of 2018 ends here! Eika and I feel truly grateful for all the experiences over the past 52 weeks, and the discussion space for this week has been REFLECT AND TURBOCHARGE.

Bestselling author and blogger Tim Ferriss recently wrote about the value of reflection and learning: 'Forget New Year's Resolutions and Conduct a "Past Year Review" instead.'

We think of this week as 'the RedPill of the RedPills' and reflect on the Why-How-What of our fantastic 52 weeks' learning journey.

Many of our friends have asked us a couple of questions on this.

- **WHY did we do the RedPills?**
  The answer is simple. We are a curious couple who believes in continuous learning and reflection, and we wanted to hyper-learn with discipline and passion. We learnt that simple changes to our lifestyles could create dramatic positive impacts into our lives. Friends (and strangers who became friends) generously shared their life hacks with us, greatly enriching our RedPills learning journey. And so, the WHY or the purpose of RedPills has really connected with people.

- **HOW did we manage the time and resources for the 52RedPills?**
  We conducted a time audit at the beginning of 2018 and figured out how we could make choices to cut out activities and create four-six hours every week for our RedPill journey. For instance, despite being series-bingers, we deactivated our Netflix account for several months of 2018, reduced our social commitments and took shorter vacations.

It's magical how much time opens up with a time audit (implemented successfully) and with the 4:30 a.m. club philosophy (still struggling to leverage this).

We learnt that resourcefulness creates resources. And experts we reached out to gladly spent time and shared their life experiences and learnings with us.

At this stage in our lives, the white sheet exercise (given below) is highly useful for time and effort prioritisation.

The White Sheet Exercise:

**Step 1:** Take an A4 size paper. Write down one to 24 (for 24 hours in a day) horizontally on the top row, and one to 80 (average life expectancy of 80 years) vertically in the left column.

**Step 2:** Shade out the areas that correspond to the birthdays you have already celebrated. For example, since we both had celebrated our 40th birthdays that year, half of the sheet was shaded).

**Step 3:** Now shade out ten hours (the approximate time you will spend sleeping and doing daily activities per day) for the balance number of years that you have remaining. So, this meant the remaining 40 years of life in our case, from the example as above.

This will now leave your sheet white only for the time that you have at hand for the balance years of your life. The sheer physicality of seeing this on paper is certain to inspire you to make sharp choices for meaningful usage of your balance time.

- **WHAT was the need, purpose and outcome of this year-long agenda?**
  The primary motive of this exercise was for us to learn and grow, and to use our learnings to become better versions of ourselves. Well, that happened.

Another objective was to spend 'blocked-off' time as a couple on topics and conversations of mutual interest. Eika and I managed to spend a good amount of time together on this journey, which really helped turbocharge some mutual thoughts and plans for the future. What was also gratifying is that our daughters joined us for some of the RedPills, learnt from us *and* taught us, as we spent time together. A key learning was, thus, the amount of time we need to spend together as a family (still working on restricting device time).

As we reflect, we also see how our shared RedPill journey has increased the number of interesting and diverse people we know, and how rich the quality of our discussions, from mental models to ancient wisdom, have become.

**More Outcomes:** RedPills Inspiration Sessions with companies, a book on RedPills (you are holding the book in your hand!) and one-minute RedPill Capsules video series, possibly. All of this in 2019!

Did we achieve everything we had set out to deep dive and learn? Will we do a Year 2 of RedPills in 2019? The answer is no. We will, however, delve deeper into some of the 52RedPills and build those lessons into our lives.

What kept us going through 2018? Vince Lombardi' s iconic words: 'Winners never quit, and quitters never win.'

2018 has been a fantastic year and our gratitude to family, friends and well-wishers who have cheered us along on this journey – we wish you all a great life and magnificent 2020.

## TO THINK AND DO THIS WEEK

### THINK

How has the year been for you? How have you felt and how have you changed?

### DO

Prepare for the coming year. Go through all the questions you've been through all this year and all the fun things you've initiated. Now pick and prepare your own 52RedPills for next year: a long list of everything you want to explore, know more about, immerse in or simply experience. And then get cracking at it, one week at a time. Best of Luck!

Experience:

Learnings:

Challenges:

# ACKNOWLEDGEMENTS

It took a village – nay a city – to help us navigate 52 weeks of 2018 to construct our unique and exciting *52RedPills* hyper-learning adventure.

First and foremost, our deepest love and gratitude to our parents, Ma and Baba, and Amma and Papa. To our pillars of rock-solid support, our siblings, Akash, Nidhi, Eishita and Raghav. To our patient and tech-savvy daughters, Oishee and Tavishee, to whom this book is dedicated (who also created our website www.52RedPills.com in a day). And to our rockstar governess, Manisha, who held fort and supplied endless cups of 'chai' as the various 'charchas' happened. Also, lots of love and thanks to the big Chaturvedi clan across the globe and the Banerjee family across India and the US.

*52RedPills* relied on our research and a lot of valuable inputs, advice and nuggets from our experts across diverse fields helping us become healthier, wealthier and wiser. So, huge rounds of heartfelt thank you(s) to:

Arriana Huffington for secrets of good sleep; Dr Marcus Ranney for introducing us to the Thrive Global community; Kunal Shah for a fabulous conversation over a coffee catch-up turned lunch; Anuj Rakyan for sharing his expertise on eating healthy (we now know why his Raw Pressery is such a fabulous brand); Santosh Desai for insights and culture codes as nobody else in India can share; Aravind Chaturvedi (IPS) and Captain Bhavesh Misra for sharing their learnings on managing situations of life and death; Brigadier Rajnish Talwar for showing us the divine in human; Sougat Ghosh and Manisha Lath Gupta for tips on the organic food chain and stories of being urban farmers; Sahil Attar for introducing us to Shaolin Kung Fu; Piyush Pandey for his love and his wisdom and his unmatched insights and stories (his one hour meeting with us became four and would have continued had he not needed to rush to a cricket game); Shilpi and Manish Sinha of Unhotel for their affection, insights and experience; Shivam and Anavila Misra for celebration of a decade of friendship over a whiskey appreciation evening which enriched both knowledge and relationships; Sanjeev Sanyal and Smita Barooah for their knowledge and grace; Mrs Lalita and Admiral Ramdas for their unparalleled enthusiasm and energy at 80+ years and their public service and stories; MS Dhoni for sharing his top three learnings over a brief interaction at a corporate event; Surbhi Misra for her sports secrets as one of India's best squash players and now coaches; Anindita Chatterjee for sharing her globe-trotting hacks and learnings; Inderpreet Singh and Geetika Mehta for introducing us to Marie Kondo and getting us started on the 'declutter' journey; Divya Palat and Aditya Hitkari (and Magic) for their love and friendship, generosity of spirit and learnings on life and adversity; Eishita Chaturvedi for sharing her Soka Gakkai perspective and life learnings as a practising Buddhist; Sumiti and Mohit Tandon for the biggest social network discussion possible; Professor Paul Brown for his learnings on Neuroscience and his amazing personal life story; Challenger Misra for showing us the VIP Insider track at Oxford University and for several long debates on metaphysics; Anuraag Agarwal for his interpretation of the science of consciousness; Nandini Das Ghoshal for a detailed discussion and notes on Ikigai; Professor Shaunaka Rishi Das of the Oxford Centre for Hindu Studies for extensive debates and discussion on The Bhagwad Gita; Roshan Abbas for being the best orator and co-author (check out our book *Speechless*) and our go-to person; RJ Siddharth for great anecdotes and music (while doing the radio segments with Eika); Dr Mayank Badola, Professor Kirti Sharma and Dr Vishwaas Sharma for helping us with doctor introductions and with medical learnings on heart health; Ash Nath, Shibani Gharat and Avinash Pant for tips and tricks on long distance running; Sandeep Bhushan for Siddharth's best ever running photograph (clicked while jogging in the Stanford University campus); Ajay Poddar of Environics for his wisdom and advice on protection from electromagnetic radiation; Shayamal Vallabhjee for bio-hacking secrets and lively chats at Soho House, Mumbai; Nirali and Kartik Shah of Maati Baani for their good cheer, great music and experiences in global collaboration; Dr Sonali Gupta and Dr Chetna Shukla for generously sharing their medical knowledge of the human mind and body; Nitin Shreshtra for showing us how profession and passion can coexist and flourish so brilliantly; Veetika Deoras for kinship and learnings over good coffee; Anjali Gulati, Sunita Wazir and Priyadarshini Gupta for evangelizing 52RedPills via diverse corporate workshops; Shreya Pilani and the TOSB Team for their support in shaping

52RedPills as leadership sessions for corporates; Gaurav Kapur for seeing the potential for 52RedPills as a video series in 2020; Neha Ahuja for proposing to us to try 52RedPills as Spotify Podcasts; and Ishita Mukherjee for her affection and for connecting us with her networks to propagate our 52RedPills origin story.

A big thank you to our panel of doctors, Vaids, Rishis, Acharyas, Swamis and astrologers who have shared their knowledge and requested not to be named.

For kind recommendations for our book, we are privileged to warmly thank Leena Nair, Shri Kishore Biyani, Krithiga Reddy and Kunal Shah.

Our *52RedPills* journey took a life of its own on our social media pages on Facebook and Instagram and we would love to thank the most enthusiastic folks who cheered us, commented on and shared our posts, helped increase our networks, and encouraged us through the 52 weeks journey, Sai Nagesh, Virginia Sharma, Awantika and Sambit Mohanty, Poonam and Bhaskar Sharma, Anupriya and Amresh Acharya, Deepali and Ajit Andhare, Richa Jain and Divakar Singh, Apurva Chamaria, Anupriya and Ashok Kumar, Rachna Arora, Smita Kothuri, Preeti Desai, Rhea Motwani, Diya Kapur Misra, Amrita Kumar, Trishna and Diptakirti Chaudhuri, Hari Ramachandran, Suparnaa Chaddha, Sapna and Vikas Kumar, Nikita and Devraj Sanyal, Susie Foxton, Avneesh Khosla, Vandana Sandhir, Kirthiga Reddy, Deepali Nair, Aditi Chaturvedi and Anurag Dhingra, Tripti and Rahul Agarwal, Priyanka and Mayur Tandon, Sonia Ratra, Anupriya Singhal, Bhaskar Das, Shipra Chaturvedi, Varun Pratap Singh, Hrishikesh Ramani, Arvinder Singh Wasu, Kedar Lele, Jeeta Das, Radhika Radia and Neelkanth Mehta of Mythopia, Aneesha, Tanmay and Pankaj (3 musketeers of Eika's Oxford gang), Taruna Upadhyaya Malik, Prachi Joshi Johar, Lulu Raghavan, Munazza Rafeek, Pooja Verma, Aparajita Bharti, Anjali and Ishaan Raina, Moneka and Deepak Khurana, Mandar Madhuri Natekar, Chitra Parthasarthy, Rahul Malhotra, Reena Daund, Artika Arora Bakshi, Sandeep Kataria, Anjali Singh, Ruchika Shrivastava Chaturvedi, Narendra Goidani, Sangeeta Jhunjhunwala, Sangeeta Multani, Saif Ahmed, Rupa Mittal, Shafali Arora, Chalaka Gajabahu, Santosh Menon, Pawan Wankhede, Vinisha Khemani Kanjilal, Ananya Sabherwal, Priya and Amarjyoti Barua, Aarti and Ankur Gupta, Nandita Sinha, Akanksha Mehta, Hirol Gandhi, Hepzibah Pathak, Akash Mehrotra, Alyna Haji Omar and Dina Omar, Amit Jain, Amith Prabhu, Prasenjeet Dutta Barua, Neha and Anil Jain, Anu Narasimhan, Anusha Shetty, Apoorva Bapna, Rajnish Chhabra, Amitesh Banerjee, Tejkaran Singh Bajaj, Debashree Dasgupta, Gayatri Yadav Harini Shankar, Professor Madhavi Narsalay, Anusha Gavankar, Madhurima Duttagupta, and Kavita Antony.

We put pen to paper on the concept of *52RedPills* in a New Years' holiday with our friends, Tarun and Monisha Katial so our warm thanks and acknowledgements to them.

In constructing the *52RedPills* book, a big thank you to our wise friend, Shayamal Vallabhjee for introducing us to Pan Macmillan India. Thank you to our dear friend, Pushpanjali Banerji (Talli Creative) for fantastic help in visualization of the original cover designs of our book. A BIG thank you to our gentle superwoman, our editor, Avneet Kaur for her dedication and alignment to our cause and essence of 52RedPills – thank you Avneet, you are an author's dream. Thank you also to our marketing whiz, Bharti Taneja for joining forces with us and spreading the good word on the book. And finally a big thank you to the entire Pan Macmillan India team who continue to passionately support the 52RedPills journey.

Thank you, folks, for all the kindness and love.

Much gratitude,

Eika and Siddharth